Lindy Smith's
MINI CAKES
ACADEMY

David and Charles

www.stitchcraftcreate.co.uk

Contents

The cakes
Vintage

Vintage

Milestones

Milestones

Childhood

Designer

Childhood

Designer

Introduction

Petite yet perfect, beautiful yet detailed, mini cakes make fabulous small gifts to be given and enjoyed. These miniature sweet treats have always appealed to me, they are very personal yet far less daunting to bake and decorate than a large cake. I love experimenting with colour, patterns and design and mini cakes make an ideal canvas on which to try out my ideas. The cakes in this book cover a wide range of themes under four chapter headings: vintage, milestones, childhood and designer. I think the cakes make quite an eclectic mix, so I trust I have included ones that will appeal and inspire you.

I am particularly thrilled with the Hundertwasser-style Happy Home cake. This was a design that just popped into my head, in a flash, and one I hastily scribbled on a scrap of paper before it vanished – sometimes designs come to me like this. I also love the Autumn Magic cakes that were inspired by the countryside around my new home in the Shropshire hills. The two designs for this project were researched, considered, planned and developed over a few weeks during the autumn but never the less are just as effective and unique all year round. Another favourite is the Graduation Honours cake, created for my daughter. For me it was a real privilege to create this special cake for her. She has grown up surrounded by my cakes and books and is the one person I can completely rely on to give me an honest opinion.

Throughout the book I have used a selection of cake sizes from the almost bite-sized 5cm (2in) to larger 7.5cm (3in) cakes, ideal for sharing. The size you select is entirely up to you. My students vary hugely in their opinions as to the perfect size. For a mini cake I prefer smaller but I'm often outnumbered! For those of you who enjoy sculpting cakes, I've included a number of designs ranging from seaside beach huts for sunny summer days to oriental paisleys for a touch of the exotic. All are achievable using the templates supplied within the project pages. The designs contained within these pages do not only work on mini cakes, so why not try up-scaling them into larger celebration cakes or even multi-tiered wedding cakes? I've created an example for the rosette mini cakes to show you how this is possible.

I believe inspiration is vital, so for each cake I have put together a collection of items, including my own photos, and created mood-boards based around colour and theme. My intention is to start you thinking, to spark ideas to help you on your own journey of discovery. If you are new to cake decorating this may seem like a leap in the dark but I assure you, once you have followed the instructions in this book and are feeling more confident with your sugarcraft techniques, you'll be able to adapt and change my designs to suit.

As always, I love to see how I've inspired you, so please do add pictures of your creations to Pinterest, quoting my name or this book so I can easily find them, or Tweet on Twitter using my Twitter handle @LindysCakes or post onto the Lindy's Cakes Facebook page.

To see more of my decorated mini cakes and to gather inspiration, please visit my website where there is a wealth of examples just waiting for you to discover. Click on the galleries, the blog and the shop to see cakes in all shapes, sizes and colours. Please note all the specialist equipment and tools you will need to create the cakes in this book are available via the online shop on my website.

I hope you find this book an inspiration.
Happy sugarcrafting

www.lindyscakes.co.uk

Introducing mini cakes

Whether they are cute and adorable or bite-sized packages of sophistication, baking and decorating mini cakes is always enjoyable. There is no pressure, you can experiment with design and colour and if you're not happy with the result it really doesn't matter as you can always have another go. I baked and decorated my first mini cakes over a decade ago by cutting up larger cakes. Today, however, we are spoilt as purpose-made round and square multi-mini tins and shaped bakeware are readily available, making baking and covering mini cakes so much easier.

So what is a mini cake? For me it has to be a small cake, designed to be consumed in just a few delicious bites. I'm particularly drawn to cakes baked in 5cm (2in) round tins, but the size you select is entirely up to you and very much personal choice. I know from my students that we differ hugely in our opinions as to the perfect size, you may prefer slightly larger cakes, say 6.5cm (2.5in) cakes or even cakes as large as 10cm (4in).

Your choice of size will also be influenced by the decoration you plan to use, and the occasion. Some designs, for example my Marvellous Marigolds, call out to be placed onto tiny dainty cakes whilst others, like the Rainbow Love cake need to make more of a bold statement. I suggest you experiment with various sizes to see which you prefer working with and find the one that appeals most to you.

Look out for the handy quantities chart in the Basics section of this book, which will help you to work out how much sugarpaste (or marzipan) you need to cover the number of mini cakes you have chosen to make.

Up-scaling mini-cake designs

The designs contained on these pages not only work on mini cakes, so why not try up-scaling them onto larger celebration cakes or even multi-tiered wedding cakes. Here I have created an example for the rosette mini cakes to show you one possibility (pictured below).

Timeless Pocket Watch

A clock cake is a wonderful way to celebrate the passing of time and what could be more endearing than an attractive pocket watch? Small and beautifully finished, a pocket watch is a true piece of craftsmanship that fits comfortably into the palm of your hand. As a child I remember being entranced by my grandfather's pocket watch. Being allowed to carefully open the back to see the decorative splendour of the hand-wound movements was a real treat. Although these timepieces are part of history, falling out of fashion during the early twentieth century, a pocket watch remains evocative of the passing of years and a perfect way to mark a special anniversary.

Antique clock face with Roman numerals and elegant ornate details

A regularly used fob watch, belonging to my neighbour Bob, on its beautiful old chain

A French clock face has been used as a decorative element on this drawer knob

Creating the Timeless Pocket Watch Cake

My cake version of this classic timepiece uses a stencil and embosser to add the intricate artisan details, plus edible paints and dusts to simulate the patina of age and beauty. If you are making a version of this mini cake for a special birthday, remember to set the hands to the appropriate hour!

You will need

MATERIALS
* **cake:** 6.5cm (2½in) round mini cake
* **sugarpaste (rolled fondant):** ivory
* **modelling paste:** brown (coloured to match the bronze dust) and small amount of black
* buttercream
* white vegetable fat (shortening)
* bronze edible lustre dust (SK)
* royal icing
* **paste colours:** black and brown – a mix of Autumn Leaf (SF) and Chestnut (SF)
* pastillage
* sugar glue

EQUIPMENT
* **cake board:** 6cm (2⅜in) hardboard round cake board, or cut a larger board to size
* **templates:** clock face and oval ring
* **stencil:** gem pendent (DS)
* **cutters:** 9cm (3½in) circle, Lindy's smallest scallop diamond (LC)
* **piping tubes:** no.16, 18 and 0 (PME)
* cocktail stick (toothpick)
* spacers, 5mm (¼in) and 1mm (¹⁄₃₂in) (both LC)
* small natural sponge
* ruler
* embossing stick, side design set 2 (HP)
* craft knife
* sugar shaper and round discs
* glass-headed dressmakers' pin
* scriber
* piping bag
* paintbrush
* palette knife
* templates

See Suppliers for list of abbreviations.

The oval ring

1 Colour a small amount of pastillage to match the edible bronze lustre dust using the brown paste colours.

2 Add a little white vegetable fat to the pastillage, to prevent the paste getting too sticky. Next dunk the paste into a container of cooled boiled water and knead to incorporate. Repeat until the paste feels soft and stretchy, but don't add too much vegetable fat to the pastillage otherwise the paste will not harden.

3 Insert the softened paste into the barrel of the sugar shaper, add the medium round disc and reassemble the tool. Push the plunger down to expel the air and pump the handle to build up pressure until it 'bites'. The paste should squeeze out easily and smoothly, if it does not the consistency is probably incorrect so remove the paste and add some more white vegetable fat or water.

Tip
Pastillage is brittle so why not make a spare just in case!

4 Place a squeezed out length of paste over the oval template (see the end of this project), so the join is on one of the long sides **(A)**. Cut to fit using a craft knife. Leave to dry thoroughly in a warm place. An airing cupboard is ideal if you have one, or place the pastillage in a warm oven that has been switched off – you are aiming to remove the moisture from the paste.

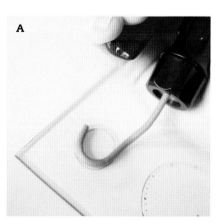

A

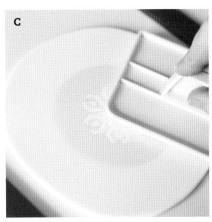

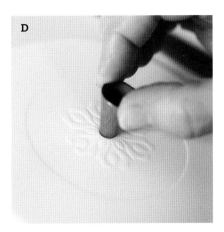

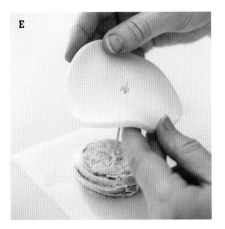

Shaping and covering the watch

1 Freeze the mini cake, as this will allow you to slice and shape the pocket watch more easily.

2 Slice the frozen 6.5cm (2½in) mini cake horizontally into 1.5cm (⅝in) slices. You will be able to cut three or four slices per cake.

Tip

You may find it easier to use a small pair of scissors to shape the cake rather than a knife.

3 Take one slice of cake and, while it is still frozen, use a small knife and carefully remove a 5mm (¼in) wedge from the base of the cake and from around the top to smooth out all the corners and give the cake a more typical pocket watch shape **(B)**. Place the cake on top of the 6cm (2⅜in) cake board using buttercream to secure. Allow the cake to completely defrost.

4 Roll out a 10cm (4in) or larger circle of ivory sugarpaste between 5mm (¼in) spacers. Place the gem pendant stencil in the centre of the sugarpaste, then with a smoother press down to force the soft sugarpaste up to the upper surface of the stencil **(C)**. Carefully remove the stencil.

5 Centrally position a 9cm (3½in) pastry circle cutter over the design and cut out a circle of textured paste. Remove the centre of the paste using a number 16 piping tube as a cutter **(D)**, keeping the small circle of paste removed.

6 Insert a cocktail stick vertically into the centre of the cake top then spread a thin layer of buttercream over the cake.

7 Carefully pick up the textured sugarpaste and position the central hole of the design over the cocktail stick, carefully lower the textured sugarpaste onto the cake **(E)** – this ensures that the pattern is placed accurately in the centre of the cake. Ease in the sugarpaste at the base of the cake and trim as necessary, using a palette knife.

8 Remove the cocktail stick and replace with the small sugarpaste circle removed earlier. Next take the wider end of a PME piping tube and remove a disc of sugarpaste from the cake to make the seconds dial **(F)**. Replace this disc with one of the same size but cut from 3mm (⅛in) thick sugarpaste. Allow the sugarpaste covering to crust over.

Tip

If only making one cake, slice and carve a few then choose the best.

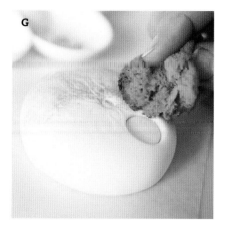

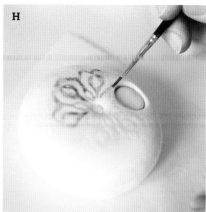

Painting

Dilute the chestnut paste colour with clear spirit (eg gin or vodka) or cooled boiled water then, using a damp natural sponge, stipple the diluted colour over the watch face **(G)**. Take a paintbrush and using a darker colour, paint around the edge of the seconds dial and the edge of the pattern as shown **(H)**. Allow the paint to dry. Then, take a damp sponge and use to remove some of the paint to help highlight the pattern.

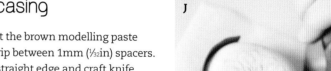

The casing

1 Roll out the brown modelling paste into a strip between 1mm (1/32in) spacers. Using a straight edge and craft knife cut a 2cm (¾in) wide strip **(I)**. Starting at the top of the watch, the opposite side to the seconds dial, wrap the strip around the sides of the cake. Cut to fit and secure in place with sugar glue **(J)**.

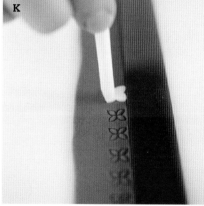

2 Roll out another thin strip of brown modelling paste. Place a 5mm (¼in) spacer along the length then, holding the embossing stick between your thumb and forefinger, place one side of the embosser against the spacer and press down onto the paste to emboss, repeat leaving 5mm (¼in) intervals along the strip **(K)**.

3 Cut out the embossed strip by taking a straight edge and craft knife and cutting 1mm (1/32in) from either side of the line of embossed pattern. Starting at the top of the watch again, position this embossed strip in the centre of the first strip and wrap around the cake as before.

4 Soften some brown modelling paste with white vegetable fat and water, as prepared for the pastillage, and place together with the small round disc inside the sugar shaper. Squeeze out a length of paste and place around the top of the casing to create a border for the watch face **(L)**.

Tip

Try to do the paint effect on the watch face quickly and efficiently so that the pattern doesn't dissolve or get rubbed away.

> **Time you enjoy wasting is not wasted time.**
>
> Marthe Troly-Curtin

The watch face

1 Place the clock face template (see the end of this project) onto the cake, aligning the 12 o'clock position with the join in the casing. Secure by inserting a glass headed dressmakers' pin into the centre of the template. Using a scriber and the template as a guide, mark the position of the hours onto the cake **(M)**. Remove the template and the pin.

2 Roll out the black modelling paste between 1mm (⅛in) spacers and cut out six scalloped diamonds. Using a craft knife, cut away two points from each shape and attach these points to denote the hours around the edge of the watch face **(N)**.

3 Reposition the template and mark the minutes around the edge of the face. Colour some royal icing black and place inside a piping tube together with the PME no. 0 piping tube. Pipe small dots over the marked minutes **(O)**. Pipe additional dots onto the face of the seconds dial, this time by eye.

4 Pipe the Roman numerals, positioning them freehand between the textured pattern of the watch face and the marked hour positions. Use the photograph of the finished cake for guidance and note that, for this watch, the numerals IV – VIII change direction!

5 For the tip of the watch hands roll small balls of black paste and elongate each by rolling backwards and forwards over one side with your finger. Place onto the cake. Then roll very thin sausages of paste and attach in place to complete each hand. Add a couple of flattened balls to the centre of the watch and also to the centre of the seconds dial.

M

N

O

The watch stem and crown

1 Roll a 1cm (⅜in) wide ball of brown modelling paste, flatten a little and attach to the top of the watch, over the join in the embossed trim. Indent the top of the ball with a paintbrush and place the join in the dried oval pastillage ring into the space created using a little royal icing to secure. Support the ring with a little kitchen paper while the royal icing dries.

2 For the crown, roll a 1.25cm (½in) ball of brown modelling paste, hold it between your thumb and forefinger and make parallel vertical cuts around the ball **(P)**. Top with a small disc cut from thinly rolled modelling paste using a no.18 piping tube and attach in place.

3 Add two hand-rolled 2cm (¾in) long sausages below the crown on either side of the pastillage oval.

4 Finally, add a ring of paste around the base of the stem using a sugar shaper filled with the small round disc and softened brown modelling paste. Allow to dry.

5 Once all the elements of the pocket watch have set. Mix edible lustre dust with boiled water and paint over the watch casing, stem and crown. You may need a couple of coats **(Q)**.

Tip

I have tried many different edible metallic finishes but the ones from Squires give me the most vibrant and reflective finish. Using a dust also means that I can ensure that the paint is not too thick and so doesn't fill the embossed patterns.

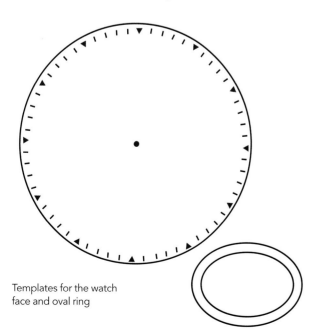

Templates for the watch face and oval ring

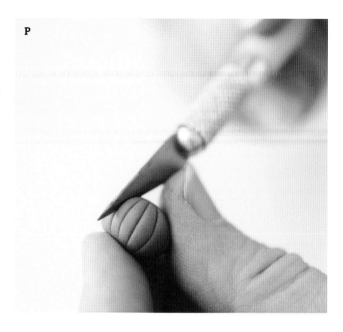

Elegant watch wheel cakes

Cog wheels and watch gears are easy to make – simply use stencils to add texture and small cutters to create the intricate shapes. These are ideal cakes for steampunk enthusiasts.

You will need

* **mini cakes:** in a selection of sizes
* **sugarpaste (rolled fondant):** sage green, dusty blue and slate blue/grey
* paste colours of your choice to paint the cakes
* **pastillage**
* **edible lustre dusts:** light silver (SK), antique gold (SK) and bronze (SK)
* **stencils:** a selection with circular patterns
* **cutters:** circle cutters plus cutters and round piping tubes to remove shapes from inside and outside of the wheels
* **embosser** as for the main cake
* flat headed paintbrush
* glass-headed dressmakers' pins

1 Roll out some pastillage and emboss it using a stencil, as for the main cake. Cut out a circle so the pattern is in the centre. Then using a selection of cutters remove shapes from around the outside edge of the circle and from areas inside the circle, using the photograph as guidance. Place on a foam pad to dry. Repeat to make a selection of different sized wheels. Also, for each mini cake, create one wheel from which a quarter segment has been removed. Once thoroughly dry, paint with edible lustre dust as for the main cake.

2 Cover the cakes with the different colour sugarpastes and add the occasional embossed pattern, using the embosser used on the main cake. Allow the sugarpaste to crust over.

3 Dilute appropriate paste colours in boiled water or clear spirit and using a flat headed paintbrush, paint over the cakes with sweeping strokes in different directions, until you are happy with the effect. Allow the paint to dry overnight.

4 Attach the wheels to the cakes using royal icing to secure and dressmakers' pins to temporarily hold them in place. Remove the pins once the royal icing is dry.

Tip

Make your pastillage cog wheels well in advance to allow them plenty of time to dry.

Bonny Beach Huts

Colourful beach huts, for many of us, evoke nostalgic childhood memories of wonderful days spent by the seaside, building sandcastles, splashing around in the shallows and discovering sea life in amazing rock pools. When I was young, my grandparents owned a beach hut at Sutton-on-Sea on the east coast of England. I remember being entranced by this delightful little home from home, from the singing kettle to the net curtains on the windows. The inside of the hut I remember as having a cheerful white and yellow colour scheme but the outside was, if I remember correctly, a lot darker perhaps, dark blue or green. Styles and colours of beach huts around the British coast vary enormously, in some locations the huts are all the same while in others there is a much more haphazard approach.

A wonderful assortment of beach huts at
Wells-next-the-Sea on the Norfolk coast

Shop windows are always a good source of
cake inspiration – here a beach hut money box

Creating the Bonny Beach Hut Cakes

For my beach hut cakes I've been inspired by the wonderful eclectic and sometimes eccentric mix of little huts at Wells-next-the-Sea, on the north Norfolk coast. I have taken two basic shapes and decorated them in different ways. The following instructions will tell you how to make the blue and yellow hut, and I've also explained how to vary the details to make the other two. I hope this will inspire you to create your own personalized cakes.

You will need

MATERIALS
- **cake:** 15cm (6in) square
- **sugarpaste (rolled fondant):** white, yellow, navy blue, mid-blue, green, orange and three shades of grey
- **modelling paste:** yellow, navy blue, mid-blue, green, orange, three shades of grey, black and white
- buttercream or ganache
- sugar glue
- soft brown sugar

EQUIPMENT
- **cake boards:** 5 x 6cm (2 x 2⅜in) hardboard rectangles, you may need to cut a larger cake board to size
- carving knife
- 10cm (4in) waxed paper squares, one per beach hut
- spacers, 5mm (¼in) and 1mm (¹⁄₃₂in) (both LC)
- smoothers x 2, both with one straight edge
- cocktail sticks (toothpicks)
- set square
- craft knife or palette knife
- **cutters:** multi ribbon cutter (FMM), small diamond cutter (LC)
- cutting wheel (PME)
- scissors
- piping tube
- beach mould set AM018 (AM)
- templates

See Suppliers for list of abbreviations.

Carving the cakes

1 Make two paper templates (provided at the end of this project) for each hut.

2 Level the cake to a height of 6cm (2⅜in), and place one of the templates on top, securing it in place with cocktail sticks (toothpicks). Take a carving knife and cut vertically around the template **(A)**.

3 Attach the second template to the other side of the cake with cocktail sticks, ensuring the templates are perfectly aligned, and use it to adjust your carved shape to ensure that it is perfectly symmetrical. Repeat to create as many huts as you wish. You will be able to cut all three huts from the 15cm (6in) square cake.

4 Attach each hut to a hardboard base using buttercream.

Covering the hut

1 Knead the navy blue sugarpaste to warm, then roll out to a depth of 5mm (¼in) using spacers. Cut two straight edges at right angles to each other then, using a set square and a craft knife, mark 5mm (¼in) intervals as shown **(B)**. Take a straight edge, I am using my 1mm (¹⁄₃₂in) spacers, and indent vertical lines on the paste to create the vertical cladding **(C)**.

2 Carefully pick up the paste and place it onto a waxed paper square, flipping the sugarpaste over so the underside is uppermost.

3 Cover the back of the cake hut with a thin layer of buttercream, then carefully place the buttercreamed surface on top of the rolled out sugarpaste. Using a palette knife, cut the navy blue sugarpaste to size, ensuring that the palette knife is flush with the cake to achieve a straight cut **(D)**.

4 Place the cake upright on its base and, if necessary, adjust the embossed vertical cladding using the set square. Next cover the front of the hut with buttercream and white sugarpaste using the same method but without embossing the cladding.

Tip
The sugarpaste for the front of the hut doesn't need
to be embossed as all the details
are made from modelling paste.

A

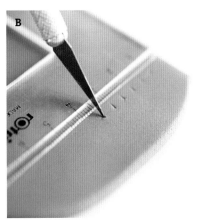

B

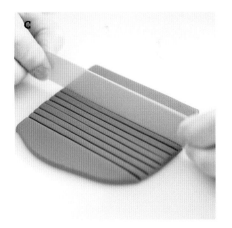

C

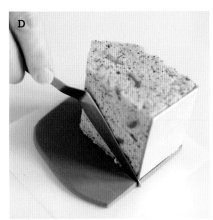

D

VINTAGE

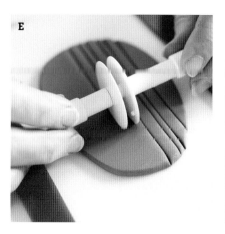

E

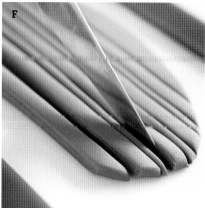

F

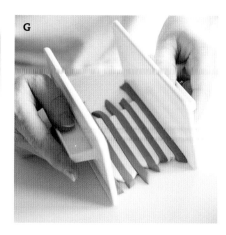

G

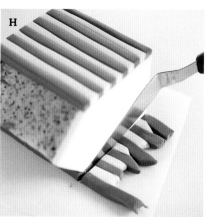

H

I

J

5 Separately, roll out the yellow and navy sugarpaste between 5mm (¼in) spacers. Using the multi ribbon cutter set to a width of 7mm (⁵⁄₁₆in), cut a series of strips from each colour **(E)**. Only cut halfway through the paste with the cutter, otherwise the tool will mark the strips, and complete the cut with a craft knife or palette knife **(F)**.

6 Pick up strips of each colour and place them adjacent to one another on your work board, and continue adding alternate stripes until you have a width of 7cm (2¾in). Take the smoothers and gently push the strips together so that they stick together securely **(G)**.

7 Carefully pick up the paste and place it onto waxed paper, flipping the sugarpaste over so the underside is uppermost. Cover one side of the cake hut with a thin layer of buttercream, then place in position on the striped sugarpaste so that the stripes run horizontally along the side of the hut. Cut away the excess sugarpaste, ensuring that the cuts are flush with the front and back of the cake and corners remain sharp. Repeat for the remaining side **(H)**.

8 Take a smoother and place it on one side of the roof, press down gently to ease the sugarpaste walls in line with the roof as shown **(I)**. Repeat for the second side.

9 Roll out one of the grey sugarpastes between spacers and cut two rectangles slightly larger than each side of the roof. Mine are 7.5 x 5cm (3 x 2in) but yours may be slightly larger or smaller so do check. Attach in place with buttercream as shown **(J)**.

10 Using a smoother, roll a sausage of grey sugarpaste **(K)** and attach it to the join between the roof sections. Squeeze into shape to form a ridge by using two smoothers. Trim the ends to fit. Allow your covered hut to firm up.

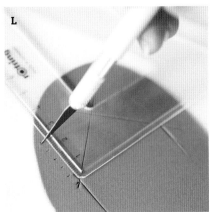

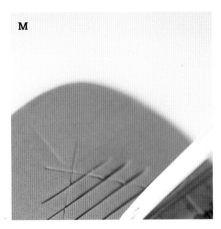

Adding the front

1 Thinly roll out the navy blue modelling paste between 1mm (¹⁄₃₂in) spacers. Place the hut template onto the paste and cut around the pitched roof. Place the set square over the lowest points of the roof as shown, and mark the paste at 5mm (¼in) intervals using a craft knife **(L)**.

2 Using a straight edge and a cutting wheel cut the paste for the front section of the roof into horizontal 5mm (¼in) wide strips **(M)**. Attach in place with sugar glue. Separately roll out the navy blue and yellow modelling paste and cut into 5mm (¼in) wide strips using a cutting wheel. Next arrange these vertically on the front of the hut as shown using sugar glue to secure **(N)**. Add a thinner vertical central strip to separate the doors and a horizontal 'drip board' above.

3 Roll out a small amount of black modelling paste and cut 5mm (¼in) hinges and bolts and attach in place, referring to the photograph for guidance **(N)**.

Adding the roof

1 Roll out one of the grey modelling pastes between the 1mm (¹⁄₃₂in) spacers and cut out a rectangle the same width as your hut's roof (about 7.5cm/3in) and the same length as the distance over the roof and under the eaves (about 12cm/4¾in). Carefully drape the strip over the roof of the hut. Tuck the ends under the eaves and trim with a craft knife if necessary **(O)**.

2 Take a straight edge and emboss a horizontal line half way down either side of the roof to look as if the roofing felt is over lapping **(P)**.

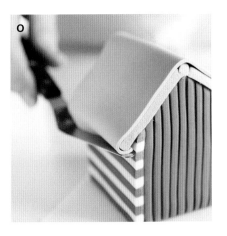

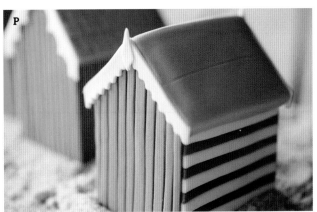

> Small is beautiful.
>
> E· F· Schumacher

3 For the decorative fascia on the gable ends, fit the multi ribbon cutter with one of the wavy discs and one straight disc, setting the wheels at around 9mm (⅜in) apart. Roll out the yellow modelling paste between 1mm (¹⁄₃₂in) spacers and cut four wavy strips as shown **(Q)**.

4 Attach one strip in place using sugar glue, trim the apex using a craft knife and shape the lower end using a small pair of scissors. Repeat for the other three strips. To finish the roof cut two small diamonds using the small cutter and attach in place at the centre of the apex.

Decorating the other huts

Take inspiration from my beach huts, and use the techniques described above to decorate your own, but change the colours and styles as desired. For example, vary the roofs by cutting and applying textured strips of paste in slightly different colours. You can also have fun with the gable ends making them highly decorative, or leaving them plain. For the orange hut I have used the embossing method all around the hut to make vertical cladding. Feel free to experiment and be adventurous. Display your cakes on a layer of soft brown sugar – it looks just like sand. Add a few finishing touches, such as the flippers (below) made using left-over modelling paste and a beach mould set.

Q

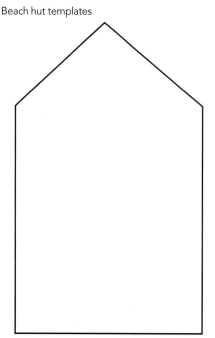

Beach hut templates

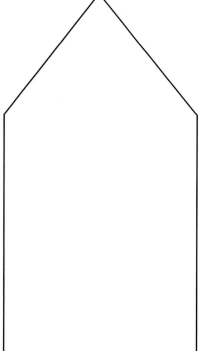

Sandcastle cake

Building a sandcastle is an essential part of a trip to the beach, but it's also very easy to build your own edible version using a mini cake, sugarpaste and soft brown sugar.

VINTAGE

You will need

* **cake:** 2.5cm (1in) mini cake baked in a multi-mini tin
* **sugarpaste (rolled fondant):** golden brown
* **modelling paste:** orange and black
* soft brown sugar
* 12.5cm (5in) cake board
* cocktail stick (toothpick)
* craft knife
* small plastic bottle top/lid

1 Place some soft brown sugar into a bowl and thoroughly mix in a ¼tsp of water using a metal spoon. The sugar should take on the appearance of slightly damp sand. Place a little of the damp sugar into the plastic bottle top using a teaspoon and press down. Flip the bottle top over and knock or squeeze the lid to release the sugar sandcastle. Make approximately 12.

2 Place the cake in the centre of the cake board, cover with a thin layer of buttercream and then cover the entire cake and board with sugarpaste. Paint over the sugarpaste with water then spoon on and pat the damp sugar over the entire cake and board. Once complete add small sugar sandcastles as shown.

3 Mark the castle entrance by adding small balls of black modelling paste. Finally, make a flag by wrapping the base of a 4 x 2.5cm (1½ x 1in) equilateral triangle made of orange modelling paste around one end of a cocktail stick. Insert the other end into the top of the castle and top with a ball of black paste. Arrange the flag so it looks as if it's fluttering in a gentle breeze. Don't forget that the flag must be removed before the cake is eaten.

Vintage Cotton Reels

Have you noticed that as part of the trend for all things vintage, wooden bobbins and cotton reels are being lovingly 'up-cycled' to create all manner of things? I have seen cotton reels covered with old-fashioned ribbon to make quirky Christmas baubles, cotton reels threaded onto colourful string and used as funky necklaces and coat racks where cotton reels have been used instead of hooks. A cotton reel is such a simple object, but it is part of our history. I have a sewing box inherited from my grandmother, which I love to riffle through as it's full of all sorts of old bits and pieces, including vintage cotton reels in all shapes and sizes and it is these that are my inspiration for this set of mini cakes.

Cotton reels in all shapes and sizes full of colourful thread – fabulous colour inspiration!

Wonderful vintage wooden cotton reels from a bygone era, complete with fascinating labels

Creating the Vintage Cotton Reel Cakes

Traditionally cotton reels were made of wood and usually incorporated the maker's label on a small printed circle at each end. I have created these cotton reel cakes by sandwiching a cake covered in edible sugar cotton between hardboard cake boards decorated to look like the wooden ends.

You will need

MATERIALS
* **cake:** 5cm (2in) round mini cake
* **sugarpaste (rolled fondant):** dark pink, pink and green
* **modelling paste:** dark pink, pink and green, brown and cream
* buttercream
* royal icing coloured deep cream
* pastillage coloured grey
* edible silver lustre dust (SK)
* sugar glue

EQUIPMENT
* **cake boards:** 7.5cm (3in) round hardboard, two per cake
* **spacers:** 5mm (¼in) and 1mm (⅟₃₂in) (both LC)
* **cutters:** circle 7.5cm (3in) and 3cm (1¼in)
* craft knife
* cutting wheel
* smoother
* sugar shaper with medium round disc and half moon disc
* lace motif stick embosser set 19 (HP)
* five point medallion stencil C322 (DS)
* palette knife

See Suppliers for list of abbreviations.

Making the pastillage needle

1 Start by kneading the grey pastillage to warm it, then roll into a 4mm (⅛in) wide sausage. Once the sausage is a uniform shape roll one end to a point using a smoother. Cut the tapered sausage to a length of 9cm (3½in) and pinch to round off the cut end. Cut the eye with a craft knife and open slightly. Place the completed needle on a foam pad to dry.

Tip
Pastillage needs to dry thoroughly to gain its strength so make sure you make this needle well in advance of decorating the cake.

2 Once dry, paint over the needle with the lustre dust mixed to a paint with water, clear alcohol or confectioners glaze.

> " If you cannot do great things, do small things in a great way. "
>
> Napoleon Hill

Making the cotton reel ends

1 These are best made in advance in stages so that there is time for the paste to dry between the steps. Knead the brown modelling paste to warm it, adding a little white fat and water if the paste is a little dry and crumbly. You want the paste to be pliable but firm.

2 Roll out the brown paste between 1mm (⅟₃₂in) spacers. Using the 7.5cm (3in) circle cutter, cut out two circles for each cake. Remove the excess paste and leave the cut-out circles on your work surface to firm up a little, to help prevent them distorting when lifted.

A

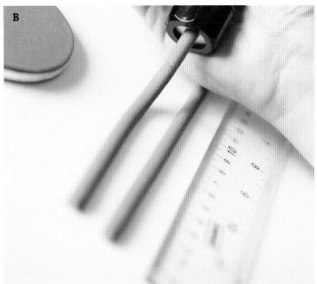

B

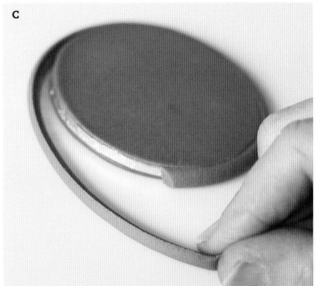

C

3 Take two hardboard cake boards per cake and paint sugar glue over one side. Carefully lift and position a brown paste circle over each board **(A)**, ensuring the paste reaches right to the very edge of the board, adjust as necessary. Leave the paste to harden.

4 Once dry, turn the covered boards over and cover the top side with another circle of brown paste. Again allow to dry.

5 To create the textured wooden edge of the reel, soften some of the brown modelling paste so it is really quite soft. Do this by firstly kneading in some white vegetable fat and then dunking the paste into cooled boiled water and re-kneading. Repeat until it feels soft and stretchy. Place the paste together with the half moon disc into the sugar shaper. Squeeze out 28cm (11in) lengths of paste onto your work surface (if the paste doesn't come out easily it isn't soft enough) **(B)**. You will need one for each covered board.

6 Next, take a paintbrush and paint glue over the edges of the covered boards. Make a diagonal cut across one end of each length. Then attach the lengths in place around the boards so that the flat side abuts the edges of the paste circles above and below the board **(C)**. Cut the paste to fit with a craft knife.

7 Using a cutting wheel, indent each edge with parallel diagonal marks about 5mm (¼in) apart **(D)**. Allow to dry.

D

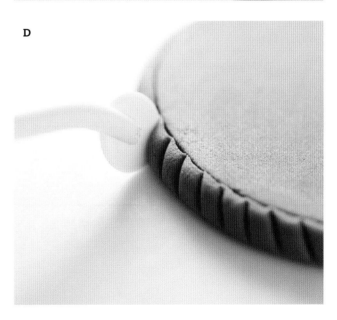

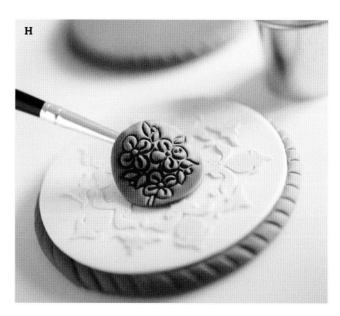

8 Next, decorate the tops of the cotton reels. Roll out the cream modelling paste, ideally between 1mm (1⁄32in) spacers. Using the 7.5cm (3in) circle cutter, cut out one cream circle per cake. Allow the paste to firm up a little, then carefully lift and position on top of half of the covered boards. These will be your cotton reel tops.

9 Place the five point medallion stencil centrally over one of the covered cream circles. Using a palette knife, carefully spread deep cream royal icing over the stencil. Use one or two strokes going from one side of the stencil to another **(E)**. Do not at any point lift the palette knife as this may cause the stencil to also lift and consequently smudge the pattern. Once the icing is of an even thickness, carefully remove the stencil **(F)**. Repeat for the other reel tops.

10 Thinly roll out a small amount of the modelling pastes that colour match your sugarpaste. Take the lace embosser and, holding it between your thumb and forefinger at right angles to the paste, press the embosser firmly into the modelling paste before releasing **(G)**.

11 Cut out embossed circles using the 3cm (1¼in) circle cutter and centrally add one to each stencilled top **(H)**.

> Nothing is too small to know and nothing is too big to attempt.
>
> William Van Horne

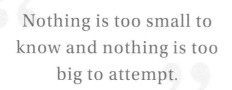

VINTAGE

Covering the cotton reel sides

1 Level your mini cake to a height equal to the diameter of the cake. If you baked your cake in multi-mini tins then this height will be the top edge of the tin.

2 Carefully cover just the sides of the cakes with a thin layer of buttercream to act as glue for the sugarpaste.

3 Knead the pink sugarpaste to warm it and then roll it out into a 22cm (8½in) long strip using 5mm (¼in) spacers. Turn the paste over and cut the strip to a width of 5cm (2in). Place the cake on its side on top of the strip, aligning the top and bottom of the cake with the cut edges. Roll up the cake in the paste **(I)**.

4 Where the two sides of the sugarpaste meet, trim the paste to create a neat join and rub closed using the heat of your fingers – note the join is disguised by the decoration.

5 Turn the cake upright and place the cake onto one of the covered bases using buttercream as glue.

6 Cover the top of the cake with a thin layer of buttercream to prevent it from drying out.

Adding the thread and needle

1 To create the thread, soften some of the pink modelling paste so it is really quite soft, using white vegetable fat and water as before (see Tip). Place the paste, together with the medium round disc, into the sugar shaper. Beginning at the base of the cotton reel, squeeze out the paste and wrap around the cake in a continuous spiral **(J)**. You will find you will have enough paste for about half the cake. Refill the sugar shaper and continue where you left off, until you reach the top of the cake. Repeat for the remaining cakes using the other sugarpaste colours.

2 For the cake with the needle, once you have reached the halfway point carefully pick up the pastillage needle and stick in position on one side of the cake using sugar glue. Continue to wrap the thread by placing two strands over the needle and the following one under the needle. You may have to hold the needle away from the surface of the cake for a moment so that you can continue to wrap neatly, before placing it back in position.

Tip

Modelling paste needs to be quite soft to pass through a sugar shaper. To make it sufficiently pliable, knead in some white vegetable fat and then dunk the paste into cooled boiled water and re-knead.

3 Once you have a continuous thread in place, take two lengths of paste and attach them from the top of the cake to either side of the needle eye as shown **(K)**.

4 To complete the cotton reels add the stencilled tops, attaching them in place with a little more buttercream if necessary.

Tip
For your cotton reels, choose colours that appeal to you as it's always easier working with a colour palette that you are drawn to.

Pretty pincushion

Pincushions come in all shapes and sizes, but for my version I have simply used a standard mini cake shape and added a cushion of sugarpaste in which to insert my sugar pins.

You will need

* **cake:** 5cm (2in) chocolate mini cake
* chocolate ganache
* **sugarpaste (rolled fondant):** white and red
* **modelling paste:** white and brown, plus colours for the pin heads
* **pastillage:** grey
* edible dust colours
* sugar shaper
* lace motif stick embosser set 19 (HP)
* 1mm (¹⁄₃₂in) spacers
* Selection of small flower and leaf stencils. I have used: Lindy's peony – LC100, Lindy's cherry blossom – LC106, Chinese floral circle – LC104, Lindy's hedgerow flowers – LC203, Lindy's stylized flowers – LC110 (all LC), Japanese dogwood – C313 (DS)

1 Cover the mini cake with chocolate ganache, following the instructions in the Basics section. Once the ganache has set, cover the cake with white sugarpaste.

2 Next add a shaped dome of white sugarpaste to the top of the cake to create the cushion, blending the paste into the side of the cake.

3 Roll out the red sugarpaste and cover the cushion. Cut away the excess by making a horizontal cut around the top of the cake. Smooth the cut edge with a finger.

4 Roll out the white modelling paste, using 1mm (¹⁄₃₂in) spacers and cut into a 4.5cm (1¾in) wide strip. Stencil the strip using a selection of small flower stencils and coloured dusts. To do this, place the first stencil on the strip, press onto the stencil with a smoother just enough to help prevent it moving. Dust over a small section of the stencil, vary the intensity of colour by adding more or less dust. Carefully lift the stencil away and repeat to fill the strip, changing colours and stencil as desired. Once complete, wrap the strip around the cake cutting a neat join with a craft knife.

5 Cut out an 8mm (⅜in) wide strip of brown modelling paste and texture with the lace embosser. Attach to the cake to hide the join between the cushion and the stencilled pattern.

6 Make pins by squeezing softened pastillage from a sugar shaper fitted with a small round disc. Once dry, add small balls of paste to one end and insert into the cushion.

Fair Isle and Beyond

Mixing traditional styles with new ideas is one of the things I love doing when designing cakes, and often I find my inspiration close to home. In this case it was pair of gorgeous colourful knitted slippers that really appealed to me. I later realized that the knitted pattern was a modern take on a traditional Fair Isle design. This style is often seen on knitted sweaters and is named after the tiny island where it originated, which lies halfway between Shetland and Orkney, off the Scottish coast. It was whilst I was researching 'Fair Isle' that I discovered other patterns and styles. So I decided to create two cakes, one with a Fair Isle theme and one with an folk art patterns, to show you what else is possible using the same design process. I hope my sugar interpretation of these lovely patterns inspires you to create your own.

Cosy slipper boots decorated with lines of repeating patterns

Inspiration is all around us — even on our feet! In this case, knitted slippers.

Knitwear is a great source of ideas for folk art patterns

A woolly winter hat inspired by Fair Isle patterns

Creating the Fair Isle Cakes

These two pretty cakes are simply covered with sugarpaste and then a band of grid embossed modelling paste is wrapped around the sides to make the canvas on which the patterns are added. The designs themselves are then created by piping small dots onto the square grid, either freehand or by referring to a paper pattern. The following instructions describe how to make the cake with the heart, the other folk art pattern is detailed at the end.

You will need

MATERIALS
* **cake:** 6.5cm (2½in) round mini cake
* **sugarpaste (rolled fondant):** dark pink and light pink
* buttercream
* **modelling paste:** cream
* **professional royal icing:** olive green, jade green, leaf green, light pink, mid pink, dusky pink and dark red-pink

EQUIPMENT
* **cake boards:** round hardboard, the same size as your cakes
* embroidery grid embosser (PC)
* spacers, 1mm (1⁄32in) (both LC)
* craft knife
* cutting wheel
* foam pad
* ruler
* piping bags x 7
* piping tube, no1 PME (optional)
* small scissors
* squared paper or printed grid from the internet
* coloured pencils or pens
* cocktail sticks (toothpicks)

See Suppliers for list of abbreviations.

Covering the cake

1 Level your mini cakes to a height equal to the diameter of the cake. If you baked your cake in multi-mini tins then this height will be the top edge of the tin. Attach the cake to a hardboard cake board the same size as the diameter of the cake using buttercream as glue.

2 Cover the cake with buttercream and sugarpaste, referring to the instructions in the Basics section. Once you are happy with the finish, place the cake to one side to dry.

Adding the grid

1 To add the grid, roll out the cream modelling paste into a long strip, using 1mm (1⁄32in) spacers.

Tip

Using spacers to roll out modelling paster results in an even thickness, for a uniform finish.

A

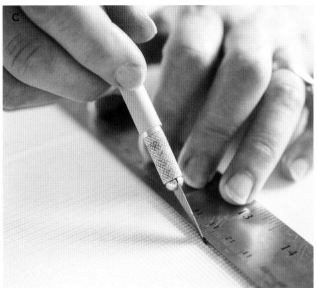

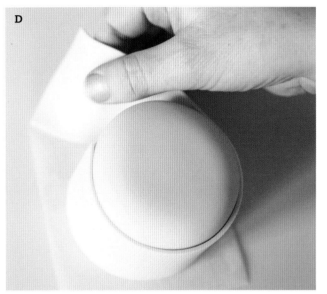

2 Allow your paste to firm up for a moment or two on your work surface as this helps to prevent the paste sticking to the embosser. Take the embroidery grid embosser and press it very firmly onto the strip **(A)**. You may find not enough pressure is applied by just pressing down on the handle, so I suggest you press firmly all over the back of the embosser with your hand. To remove the embosser, rather than just trying to use the handle, use your fingers to prise up one edge and then carefully pull away from the paste. Check that the grid has been evenly embossed, it may take a little practise!

3 Once you are happy with your first embossed grid, very carefully line up the embosser and press it into the paste for a second time **(B)**. You want the embossed grid to look continuous so it is worth taking the time to get this right. Remove as before. Using a ruler and craft knife cut out the embossed grid into a rectangle with a height of 32 squares **(C)**.

4 Paint over the sides of the cake with a little cooled boiled water or sugar glue. Carefully pick up the embossed band and wrap it completely around your cake **(D)**, making sure you do not stretch or distort the embossed grid. Where the paste band meets, take a craft knife and cut away the excess **(E)**.

> We make patterns,
> we share moments.
>
> Jenny Downham

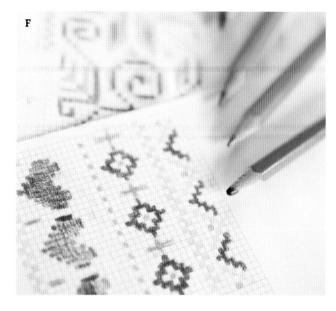

Creating your Fair Isle design

1 Take your squared paper and draw a 32 squares high rectangle or use your computer to print off grids from the internet, resizing them to match your embossed sugar grid. Choose a selection of coloured pencils or pens, I used seven colours – three greens and four pinks – but you can use as many as you wish.

2 Now begin colouring in the squares to create patterns **(F)**. Experiment with different shapes and layouts or use my cakes for inspiration. There is no need to colour the entire strip as you are just creating a counting guide so that you will know where to pipe your dots. A small section of pattern is perfectly adequate, especially if you opt for a fairly simple Fair Isle inspired design.

3 Fill a piping bag with freshly paddled light pink royal icing and snip a small hole in the tip of the bag, or use a piping nozzle in your bag if you prefer, as I have done. Starting at the base of the cake, pipe a small dot onto every other embossed square on the first row. Do this by supporting your hand, either on your work surface or other hand, and hold the tip fractionally away from the side of the cake. Squeeze the bag until the dot of icing is the required size, release the pressure and only then remove the tip, this helps avoid any unwanted peaks. Remember: squeeze, release and remove.

Tip
If a dot becomes over-sized or distorted quickly remove it with a damp paintbrush.

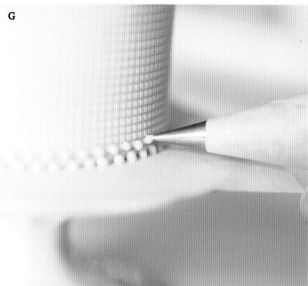

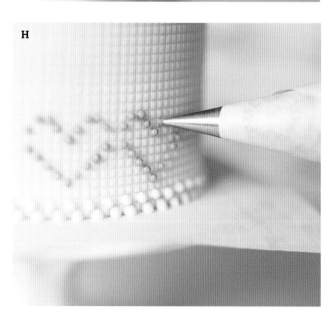

4 Once you are happy with your first row of dots (which could take a little practise, especially if you are new to piping), pipe the second row of dots as shown **(G)**.

Tip
Once you have finished with a bag of royal icing wrap in plastic to prevent the icing at the tip drying out.

5 Fill a second bag with freshly paddled dusky pink royal icing. Then, using your template to guide you, pipe the heart outlines for the row of hearts **(H)**. Count the squares carefully so they are all the same shape.

6 Once the outlines are complete, start filling in the hearts by piping dots onto alternate squares **(I)**. Doing this helps prevent the fresh dots from running into each other. Continue around the cake. Once you have gone full circle, fill in the remaining blank squares within each heart, the first set of dots should be sufficiently dry by this stage.

7 Continue working up the cake, changing colours and adding piped patterns, referring to your design and counting guide. Once complete, add a ring of piped dots to the upper edge of the cream band of embossed paste.

Creating the heart topper

1 Using your squared paper, colour squares to make yourself a heart template, my heart is 19 squares wide and 17 squares high. Take a cocktail stick (toothpick) and, using your template, prick out your heart shape as shown **(J)**.

2 Carefully cut around the pricked out heart using a cutting wheel **(K)**, neaten the curves if necessary with a craft knife. Leaving the heart on your work surface, pipe dusky pink dots around the edge and fill in the shape as before in stages. Once the royal icing has dried, carefully lift the heart and place on a foam pad and allow the paste to thoroughly dry.

3 Make a paper circle template the same size as the top of your cake. Fold the circle into quarters and unfold, where the folds meet should be the centre of your circle. Place the template on top of the cake and mark the cake's centre with a dressmakers' pin as shown **(L)**.

4 Attach the back of the dried heart to a small cocktail stick using royal icing. Once dried insert the cocktail stick into the centre of the cake. Note that the heart topper should be removed before the cake is cut.

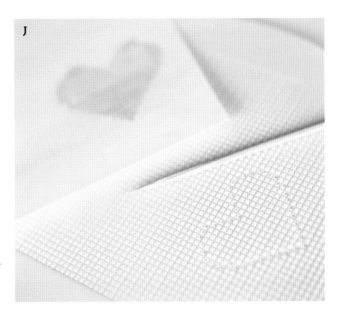

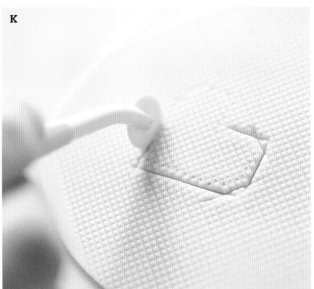

Decorating the folk art patterned cake

This cake is created in exactly the same way as the Fair Isle one, although its design is more intricate. This means that the decorative pattern is slightly harder to pipe onto the sides of the cake as the colours are not arranged in rows. However, as long as you count correctly and work on one section at a time you should find the decorating process very enjoyable and rather therapeutic!

> No act of kindness, no matter how small, is ever wasted.
>
> Aesop

Embroidered peony cake

A different decoration option is to pipe royal icing into lines rather than dots, to create an embroidered look. Simply transfer the pattern of your choice onto the cake and fill the design with coloured 'stitches', overlapping and changing colour as desired.

You will need

* **cake:** 7.5cm (3in) mini cake covered in dark cream sugarpaste
* **royal icing:** coloured as for the Fair Isle cake, plus plum
* **paste colour:** several shades of brown
* sponge
* scriber
* piping bags x 7
* template
* baking paper (parchment)

1 Dilute the brown paste colours and sponge paint the covered cake to give a mottled fabric look. Allow to dry.

2 Trace the peony design onto baking paper (parchment) then either scribe or prick the design onto the cake, using a scriber.

3 Fill your piping bags with freshly paddled royal icing. Snip a small hole in the tip of one of the green bags and start piping short lines of icing over the leaves and stems as seen in the photograph. To pipe lines touch the surface of the cake with the tip and at the same time lightly apply pressure to the bag. As the icing starts to come out, lift the tip up from the side of the cake. When the icing is of the length you need, release the pressure and place the icing down onto the cake once again. Change to another colour and continue. Repeat until the pattern is complete and you are happy with the effect.

Peony cake template
Enlarge by 200%

Prize-winning Rosettes

Whether winning 'Best in Show' or coming first in a three-legged race, there are a thousand excellent reasons to celebrate and a rosette, often awarded on such occasions, is a wonderful and lasting keepsake. Rosettes are usually made from fabric or ribbon that has been pleated or gathered to resemble a rose. These concentric layers of ruffles offer plenty of opportunities to try new textures and colour combinations, so let your creativity run riot! Why not replace the central button with a flat sugar disc and add suitable numbers or even words, if you have enough space, to personalize the cakes?

Colourful and highly decorative painted ceiling mouldings at *Norwich Cathedral, UK*

Gorgeous symmetrical pattern from the *Vairocana Buddha Prayer Wheel, Singapore*

Nature creates its own rosettes in the form of delicate blossoms

Creating the Prize-winning Rosette Cakes

For my cakes I have embellished the basic idea of a rosette by adding folded patterned circles around the edge, to give a more homemade feel. I have also introduced layers in different colours, and in the centre of each rosette I have featured a sugar button to emphasize the fabric origins of the rosettes. The following detailed instructions are for the large rosette. I have played around with the layers to make a smaller one too, just to show you some of the effects possible.

You will need

MATERIALS
* **cakes:** 6.5cm (2½in) and 7.5cm (3in) round mini cakes, ideally baked in multi-mini tins
* **sugarpaste:** pink and aqua
* buttercream
* pastillage, small amount per cake
* **modelling paste:** white, pink, dark pink, aqua blue, light aqua blue, light lime and black
* edible dusts: rose pink, lime green, blue-green
* royal icing, small amount
* sugar glue

EQUIPMENT
* **cake boards:** hardboard cake boards the same size as your cakes
* **templates:** 8cm (3¼in) and 7.5cm (3in) segmented circles, see end of project
* foam pad
* spacers, 5mm (¼in) and 1mm (¹⁄₃₂in) (LC)
* smoother
* craft knife
* paintbrushes
* **cutters:** 4cm (1½in), 3cm (1¼in) and 2.3cm (1in) circles, 38mm (1½in) and 50mm (2in) from the Five Petal Cutter set (PME), two smallest cutters from Persian Petal set 1 (LC)
* stencils: Cherry Blossom – LC106 (LC), Elegant Flower Cupcake Top Stencils – LC112 (LC)
* embossers: Flowers 1 embossing stamp set (FMM)
* button mould, patterned set AM089 (AM)
* glass-headed dressmakers' pins
* palette knife

See Suppliers for list of abbreviations.

Tip

The rosettes can be made in advance, then dried and stored until needed.

The back of the rosette

1 Copy the two eight segment circle templates (see the end of this project) and place under clear plastic. Note that the 8cm (3¼in) diameter circle is used for 7.5cm (3in) cakes and the 7.5cm (3in) diameter circle for 6.5cm (2½in) cakes.

2 Roll out the pastillage between 1mm (¹⁄₃₂in) spacers and, using the 4cm (1½in) circle cutter, cut out a disc for each rosette you plan to make. Place each disc centrally on top of a template and mark the segments using a palette knife as shown **(A)**. Quickly lift the circles and place on the foam pad to dry thoroughly. These pastillage discs are used to secure the rosettes to the mini cakes.

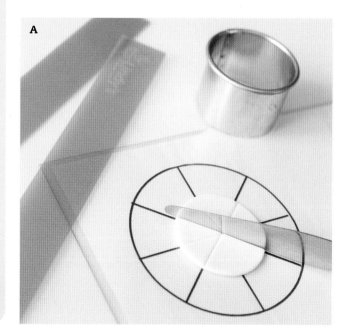

A

MILESTONES

Creating the outer patterned layer

1 Knead a small amount of white modelling paste to warm it, then roll out between the 1mm (¹⁄₃₂in) spacers. Place your chosen stencil on top of the paste. I used my elegant flower cupcake stencil but any small floral stencil of the right size should be suitable. Using a smoother gently press onto the stencil just enough to help prevent it moving **(B)**.

2 Next dip a paintbrush into the rose pink edible dust, knock off any excess then carefully dust over the petal sections of the stencil, varying the intensity of colour by adding more or less dust. Take a clean brush and dust over new sections of the pattern with lime green, taking care not to spread the green onto the pink petals. Also note that you only need to colour an area of 3cm (1¼in) diameter not the whole stencil. Finally, add the blue-green dust to the remaining sections **(C)**.

3 Once all sections are complete ensure that any excess dust is removed from the stencil to prevent any stray dust falling onto the pattern as you lift the stencil. Carefully lift the stencil away from the paste to reveal the pattern. Then take the 3cm (1¼in) circle cutter and cut a circle from the stencilled pattern **(D)**.

4 Reposition the dried pastillage circles on top of the templates and cover their tops with sugar glue. Loosely fold over part of the stencilled circle as shown and place on the pastillage disc. Create seven more stencilled circles, exactly like the first, and position to create an attractive ring of folded circles **(E)**.

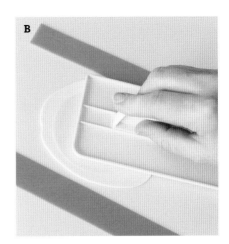

B

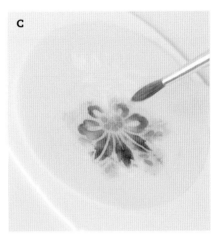

C

Tip
You can add as many different colours to your stencil as you wish, but try to use clean brushes when changing colour. Remove all excess dust between colours to ensure that your dust colours do not mix and become muddy.

D

E

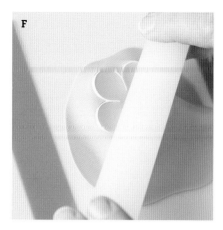

Adding the two-layer flower

1 Roll out the aqua blue modelling paste between 1mm (¹⁄₃₂in) spacers. Take the 5cm (2in) five petal cutter and, rather than pressing the cutter into the paste, lift the paste and place it over the cutting edge of the cutter. Roll over the paste with a rolling pin, this ensures that you achieve a clean cut with no untidy feathering **(F)**.

2 Run your finger over the edges of the cutter, then turn the cutter over and carefully press out the paste using a soft paintbrush. Place in the centre of the rosette, attaching it to the stencilled circles with a small amount of sugar glue.

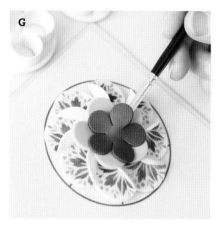

3 Repeat using the dark rose paste and the 38mm (1½in) five petal cutter. Position this smaller flower as shown, again using sugar glue to secure **(G)**.

> "Notice the small things. The rewards are inversely proportional."
>
> Liz Vassey

The black ruffle and button

1 To make the black ruffle, roll out a strip of black modelling paste between 1mm (¹⁄₃₂in) spacers and cut one edge straight using a sharp craft knife to achieve a clean line. Pick the strip up and pleat the paste as shown **(H)**.

2 Place the paste back on your work surface and trim to a width of 1cm (½in). Paint sugar glue over the centre of the rosette and carefully wind the pleated paste around to form a 2.7cm (1in) circle, as shown **(I)**.

3 Roll a ball of black paste to fill the centre of the rosette to create a platform on which to put the central button **(I)**.

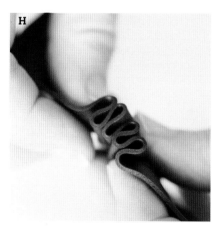

4 For the button, roll a ball of paste slightly larger than the button mould cavity and place into the mould ensuring that the sugar surface is perfectly smooth. Push the paste firmly then remove any excess with a palette knife, so the back of the mould is flat **(J)**. With your finger or a Dresden tool, ensure that the holes in the centre of the button are visible and not covered with paste.

5 Using your finger, push the back of the mould to help release the sugar button cleanly, flexing the mould this way should prevent the holes in the sugar button distorting. It may take you a couple of attempts! Attach in place with sugar glue and allow to dry.

Covering and decorating

1 Level your mini cakes to a height equal to the diameter of the cakes. If you baked your cake in multi-mini tins then the height will be the top of the tin. Attach the cakes to hardboard cake boards the same size as the diameter of the cakes using buttercream as glue.

2 Cover the cakes with buttercream and then your chosen colour of sugarpaste, referring to the instructions in the Basics section of this book. Once you are happy with the finish, place the cakes to one side to dry.

3 Place a small amount of royal icing on the back of the large rosette and attach it to the side of a 7.5cm (3in) mini cake ensuring that the holes in the button are aligned either vertically or horizontally. Use a glass-headed dressmakers' pin to temporarily hold the rosette in place.

Creating the Persian petal shapes

1 Thinly roll out the black modelling paste between 1mm (1/32in) spacers. Take the five-petal flower embosser from the embossing set and, holding it between your thumb and forefinger at right angles to the paste, press into the soft paste. Repeat seven more times, leaving space between the flowers. Next take the 2cm (¾in) wide Persian petal cutter and cut out eight shapes as shown **(K)**.

2 Using a damp paintbrush, position the cut out shapes onto the cake so it appears from the front of the cake that the shapes are a continuation of the rosette itself. Make sure that the shapes are equally spaced and adjust as necessary **(L)**. Cut the shapes to fit at the base of the cake as required.

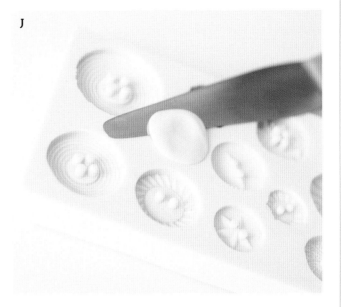

J

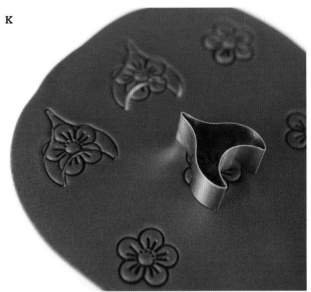

K

L

45

3 Make eight more Persian petal shapes but this time from dark rose modelling paste. Temporarily remove the rosette and stick the dark rose petals between the black ones as shown (**M**). Reapply some royal icing to the back of the rosette and attach back in place.

4 Add dark rose sugar buttons around the rosette as shown on the completed cake (**N**).

Decorating the smaller rosette cake

Make the smaller rosette in exactly the same way as the large one, but use the cherry blossom stencil and the 2.3cm (1in) circle cutter for the outer layer. To add the outer petals follow the instructions for the larger rosette, but use the smaller 1.8cm (11/16in) Persian petal cutter and the multi petal daisy embosser.

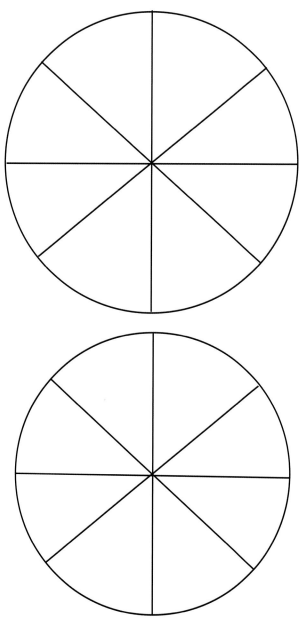

Templates for the larger (top) and smaller (bottom) rosettes

Pretty pinwheel cake

Eye-catching pinwheels are charming. Make sugar versions from squares of modelling paste with stencilled patterns.

You will need

- **cake:** 5cm (2in) mini cakes
- **sugarpaste (rolled fondant):** lime green
- **modelling paste:** black and white
- **edible dusts:** rose pink, lime green and blue green
- sugar glue
- smoother
- 1mm (⅟₃₂in) spacers (LC)
- species rose stencil (LC)
- square cutter, 5.8cm (2⅜in) from the geometric set (FMM)
- craft knife
- sugar shaper
- glass-headed dressmakers' pins

1 Roll out the white modelling paste between the 1mm (⅟₃₂in) spacers. Place the species rose stencil on top of the paste and, using a smoother, press onto the stencil just enough to help prevent it moving.

2 Using a range of edible dusts, as for the main project, dust over the stencil pattern to highlight the pattern. Carefully remove any excess dust then cut out a square shape from the patterned paste using the suggested cutter.

3 Take a straight edge, such as a spacer, and place it diagonally across the square. With the craft knife make a cut 3cm (1¼in) from one corner of the square towards the centre, repeat for the other three corners. Add some sugar glue to the centre of the square then carefully pick up one half of one of the cut corners and fold it over into the centre. Repeat the same process for the remaining corners.

4 Roll a pea-sized ball of black modelling paste and add this to the centre of the pinwheel, top this with another ball – about half the size again. Leave the pinwheel to dry.

5 Place the cake on a hardboard cake board the same size as the cake itself and cover with lime green sugarpaste.

6 To create the pinwheel's stick, add a little white vegetable fat to some black modelling paste, and then dunk the paste into a container of boiled water and knead to incorporate. Insert the softened paste into the barrel of a sugar shaper, together with the small round disc. Squeeze out the paste, then take a small length and attach it vertically to the mini cake. Attach your dried pinwheel on top using royal icing. Use a glass headed dressmakers' pin to hold the pinwheel in place while the royal icing dries.

Graduation Honours

Graduation day is a very special occasion. It is the successful culmination of years of study, hard work and exams – a memorable day full of joy and pride. Mortarboards, academic gowns, colourful hoods, degree scrolls and large celebrations mark the day at universities around the world, from Oxford to Harvard, Singapore to Mumbai. I vividly remember my own graduation day, decades ago, and now it's my own daughter Charlotte's turn – how wonderful!

Universally recognized, the mortarboard is a must on a graduation cake

Stacks of books make a great shape on which to base a cake design

Creating the Graduation Honours Cake

I have created this graduation mini cake using my daughter's favourite colour, purple, and have used ruffles of paste to gradually change the colour from purple through to gold. A symbolic mortar board has pride of place on top of the cake and is surrounded by the gold stars of success.

You will need

MATERIALS
* **cake:** 6.5cm (2½in) round mini cake
* **sugarpaste:** golden yellow, coloured using marigold paste colour (SK)
* **modelling paste:** white and black
* **paste colours:** plum, rose, marigold (all SK)
* buttercream
* sugar glue

EQUIPMENT
* **cake boards:** round hardboard, the same size as your cakes
* spacers, 1mm (1/32in) (LC)
* foam pad
* ruler
* cutting wheel
* **cutters:** 5cm (2in) square, Lindy's stylish star cutter set (LC)
* craft knife
* sugar shaper and small mesh disc
* bulbous cone modelling tool

See Suppliers for list of abbreviations.

Tip

If weather conditions are humid I suggest using pastillage instead of modelling paste for the mortarboard top. It is a much harder paste and will retain its shape for longer.

Colouring the modelling paste

Divide the white modelling paste into four. Leave one quarter white and colour the three remaining quarters, plum, rose and marigold using the paste colours suggested. Then, using these four colours, mix a complete set of fourteen graduated colours, from plum through to rose, to white and then to marigold, as shown **(A)**. Note that I have used between two and four colour changes to move from one colour to another, you can, of course, add more or less.

Preparing the mortarboard top

To prepare the top of the mortarboard, knead some of the black modelling paste to warm it, adding a little white fat and water if the paste is a little dry and crumbly. You want the paste to be pliable but firm. Roll out, ideally using 1mm (1/32in) spacers, and cut out a 5cm (2in) square. Allow to partially dry on your work surface, to prevent the shape distorting, before carefully placing on a foam pad to dry completely.

A

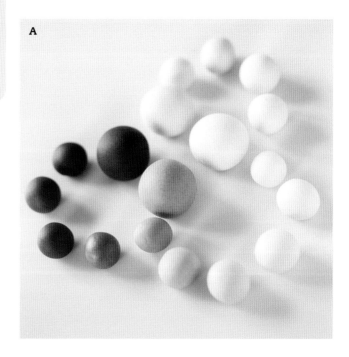

Covering the cake

1 Level your mini cake to a height equal to the diameter of the cake. If you baked your cake in multi-mini tins then this height will be the top edge of the tin. Attach the cake to a hardboard cake board the same size as the diameter of the cakes using buttercream as glue.

2 Cover the cake with buttercream and then the golden yellow sugarpaste, referring to the instructions in the Basics section. Once you are happy with the finish, place the cake to one side to dry.

Making the ruffles

1 Starting at the top edge of the cake, paint a sugar glue line diagonally down one side of the cake to 1cm (½in) above the lower edge directly opposite your starting point. Turn the cake around and paint from this point diagonally up the second side until you reach your starting point. Once you are happy that your painted glue lines are smooth and symmetrical, fill in the area below with sugar glue **(B)**. This is the area where your ruffles will be attached.

2 Knead the darkest golden yellow/marigold modelling paste to warm it, adding a little white fat and water if the paste is a little dry and crumbly. You want the paste to be pliable but firm. Roll out this paste into a long strip, using 1mm (¹⁄₃₂in) spacers. Then, using a ruler and cutting wheel, cut out a 2cm (¾in) wide ribbon of paste **(C)**.

3 Leaving the sugar ribbon on your work surface, take a bulbous modelling tool and roll back and forth along one side of the ribbon to gently thin and stretch half the width of the paste **(D)**.

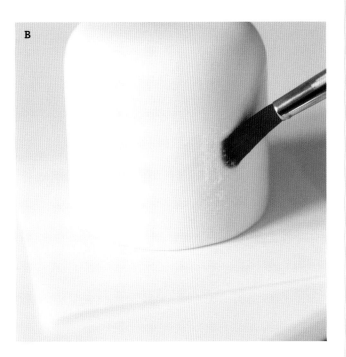

Tip
Roll and thin the edge of a modelling paste ribbon before using it to make ruffles. It is this thinning that makes the ruffles look so attractive.

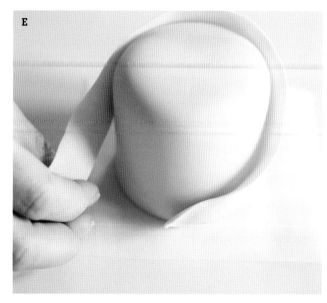

E

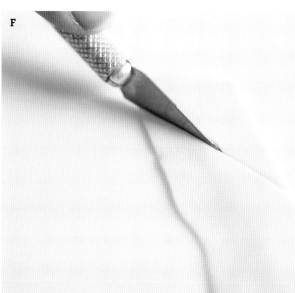

F

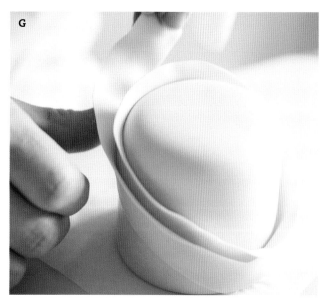

G

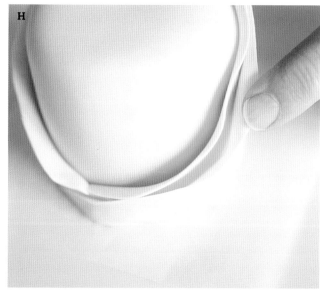

H

4 Starting at the base of the cake, wrap the paste ribbon around the cake, following the upper edge of the glued area. Position the ribbon so that the lower half is stuck to the cake whilst the upper thinned half projects above and away from the sides of the cake **(E)**. Cut away the excess ribbon length by making a neat vertical cut. Adjust the shape of the ruffle with your fingers as desired.

5 Using the next shade of modelling paste, cut and thin a second paste ribbon. Mitre one end as shown **(F)**. Starting at the base, attach this ribbon around the cake, positioning it below the first ribbon **(G)**. Cut away the excess paste by using another mitre cut, this ensures there are no unsightly blunt ends. Neatly overlap the mitred ends of the ribbon. Using your fingers, arrange the top of the second ruffled ribbon to give movement and shape **(H)**.

6 Continue adding ruffles, each time using the next shade of modelling paste, until you finish off with the plum. Note that the lengths of sugar ribbon you will need get shorter with each colour change. Place to one side to dry.

The older I get, the more I'm conscious of ways very small things can make a change in the world. Tiny little things, but the world is made up of tiny matters, isn't it?

Sandra Cisneros

MILESTONES

The mortarboard

1 Roll a 2.5cm (1in) ball of black modelling paste, cut away about a third to create a flat base **(I)**. Place this between your thumb and forefinger and squeeze to elongate the shape into an oval. Next pinch around the cut base to create sharp edges and adjust the shape of the cap **(J)**.

2 Thinly roll out the remaining black modelling paste. Then using a craft knife cut a 3mm (⅛in) wide strip of paste. Stick this around the base of the cap, using sugar glue, so the join is at the back. Trim to fit.

3 Position the cap on the top of the cake and, once you are happy with its placement, attach it using sugar glue. Add the dried black square board, made earlier, centrally to the top of the cap, adjusting its position and angle as desired.

4 Soften some of the black modelling paste so it is really quite soft. Do this by kneading in some white vegetable fat and then dunking the paste into cooled boiled water and re-kneading. Repeat until it feels soft and stretchy. Place the paste together with the smallest mesh disc into the sugar shaper. Squeeze out approximately 7.5cm (3in) lengths of paste from the sugar shaper **(K)**.

Tip

If the paste doesn't come out of the sugar shaper easily then it isn't soft enough. Take it out and repeat the softening process.

I

J

K

L

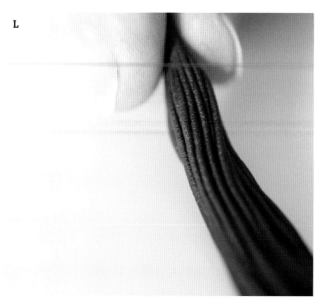

5 To make the tassel, remove the paste from the sugar shaper and twist the strands together **(L)**. Trim the twisted section to neaten and attach to the centre of the mortarboard with sugar glue, as shown on the completed cake. Trim the tassels to a uniform length using a pair of small scissors. Finally, add a small ball of black paste to the top of the mortarboard.

The stars

1 Roll out some golden yellow modelling paste between 1mm (1/32in) spacers. Using the two smallest stars from the star set, cut out approximately ten stars **(M)**.

2 Attach these around the mortarboard using sugar glue and a paintbrush.

M

That which is loved is
always beautiful.

Norwegian proverb

54

Graduation book stack

I have created this mini cake variation for graduates who still love their books, despite our computer age, and spending time in libraries. Why not personalize the spines of your stack of books with student names or the subjects they have studied?

You will need

* **cake:** 5 x 3.5 x 5cm (2 x 1⅜ x 2in)
* **sugarpaste (rolled fondant):** ivory
* **modelling paste:** black, plum, dusky pink and golden yellow
* **cake board:** rectangular hardboard, the same size as the cake (you'll probably need to cut this to size)
* palette knife
* craft knife
* **cutters:** to decorate book spines. I used the smallest cutters from Lindy's equilateral triangle set and Persian petals set 1 (both LC), and piping tubes numbers 16 and 3 used as cutters (PME)
* side design set 2, stick embossers (HP)

1 Place the cake on its cake board and cover with the ivory sugarpaste. Using a palette knife mark horizontal lines around three sides of the cake to represent the leaves of the book.

2 Separately, thinly roll out the coloured modelling paste, between 1mm (¹⁄₃₂in) spacers so the paste is exactly the same thickness. From these cut rectangles for book spines, I suggest you take your own measurements from your covered cake, and 2mm (¹⁄₁₆in) wide strips for the edges of the book covers. For the spines, start at the base of the cake and attach the cut out paste rectangles, one on top of another, up the untextured side of the mini cake. You want the top of the book spine to project 1mm (¹⁄₃₂in) above the top surface of the covered cake.

3 Cut a rectangle of paste for the cover of the top book, again taking measurements from your own cake, and attach in place so the cover abuts the top book's spine. Using a palette knife, emboss lines into the cover, adjacent and parallel to the spine, 5mm (¼in) in from the edge. This ensures the top book looks as if it can be opened! Take the 2mm (¹⁄₁₆in) strips, two for each book, and attach these horizontally to the cake to represent the edges of the stacked books.

4 Decorate the spines as desired. I used a selection of small cutters and embossers but you could paint or write on yours. Finally, create a mortarboard as for the main cake and position it on top of the cake.

Happy Home

I always like to include cakes in my books, if possible, that have been inspired by other artists. So when I discovered the amazingly colourful world of Friedensreich Hundertwasser, an Austrian artist and architect, I knew I simply had to design a cake based around his work. If you have not come across Hundertwasser, I suggest you look him up, you will no doubt be amazed! I was so drawn to his use of bright colours and unruly organic forms that this new home cake has been a delight to design and create. Hundertwasser may inspire you in a completely different way so please feel free to add your own twist to my design.

A colourful stylized landscape on a painted dish from Spain

Bird house for sale at the Christmas market in Düsseldorf, Germany

Topiary has given these trees an appealingly rounded 'lollipop' shape

Simple shapes hae been used to create this miniature building

Creating the Happy Home Cake

For my Hundertwasser inspired cake, I've taken a new home theme, as I thought it rather apt. I have placed a simple house in a Hundertwasser landscape, easily created by painting embossed icing. The stylized trees are concentric circles built up in layers, stunning yet easy to create.

> The home should be a treasure chest of the living.
>
> Le Corbusier

Covering and painting the cake

1 Level your mini cake to a height equal to the diameter of the cakes. If you baked your cake in multi-mini tins then this height will be the top edge of the tin. Attach the cake to a hardboard cake board using buttercream. Then carefully cover just the sides of the cake with a thin layer of buttercream to act as glue for the sugarpaste.

2 Knead the pale pink sugarpaste to warm it and then roll it out using 5mm (¼in) spacers. Turn the paste over and cut one edge straight. Place the cake on its side on this cut edge, aligning the top of the cake with the edge. Roll up the cake in the paste **(A)**.

3 Where the two sides of the sugarpaste meet, trim the paste to create a neat join and rub closed using the heat of your fingers. Next take a palette knife and, holding it flush with the cake board on the base of the cake, cut away the excess sugarpaste **(B)**. Turn the cake upright.

Tip

If you need to join sugarpaste, as you do here, you can easily disguise the point where the edges meet by positioning a decorative element on top.

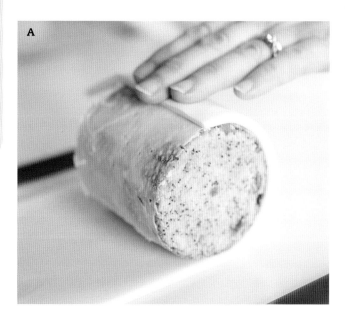

A

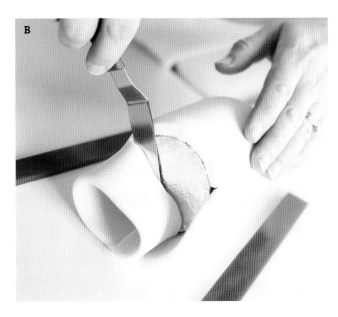

B

C

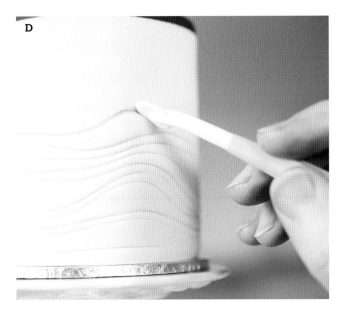

D

4 Roll out the navy blue sugarpaste between 5mm (¼in) spacers and cut out a circle of paste using the appropriate circle cutter. For a 7.5cm (3in) cake, this will be the 8.5cm (3⅜in) cutter. Cover the top of the cake with buttercream. Next place the navy paste circle on top of your cake ensuring that its edge lies flush with the pale pink sides, adjust as necessary with the help of smoothers **(C)**.

5 Working quickly so the sugarpaste does not dry out, indent the horizontal undulating bands onto the cake freehand, by carefully running a cutting wheel through the paste. Start at the bottom of the cake, varying the width of each band as you go around the cake. Note that the bands do not cross over one another. You are aiming to create the appearance of rolling countryside **(D)**.

Tip
You will probably find it easier to indent bands
if you have your cake at eye level.

6 Once you are happy with your indented pattern, add a little more interest by using the end of a paintbrush to indent lines of dots into the wider sections of the bands **(E)**. Place to one side to allow the sugarpaste to crust over before moving on.

E

Painting the cake

1 Dilute and mix the suggested paste colours with varying amounts of boiled water or clear alcohol. Choosing one colour, paint the lowest band on the cake varying the intensity of the colour applied. Also paint the indented line above the band, as this helps to enhance the texture of the paste.

2 Change colour and paint the next band up. Continue working up the cake **(F)**, selecting colours carefully as you do so, referring to the finished cake for guidance. Ensure that any indented dots are also filled with colour to help them become a visible feature. Once complete, leave to dry.

Tip

If you have applied too much paint or you change you're mind, simply remove paste colour with a clean damp brush.

Adding the house

1 Make two copies of the new home template (see below) and carefully cut away the door and roof from one and cut out the shutters from the other.

2 Individually roll out the pink, red and dark orange modelling paste colour between 2mm (¹⁄₁₆in) spacers or barbecue skewers. Place the house template on the pink paste and cleanly cut around the edges of the template using a craft knife **(G)**. Remove the excess paste but leave it on your work surface. Cut out the door from red paste and position in place, making sure it fits snugly, rub a finger over the join to help the pastes stick together. Lift the house carefully and attach it to the dried painted cake using sugar glue.

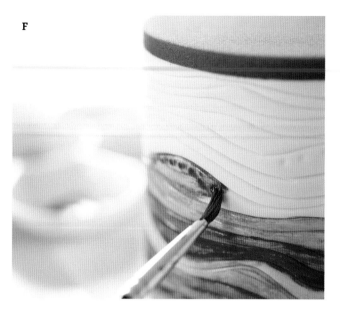

F

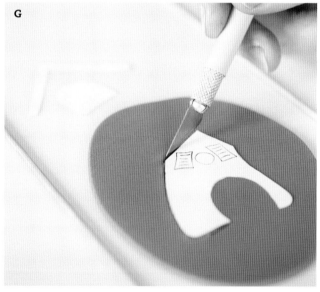

G

New home template

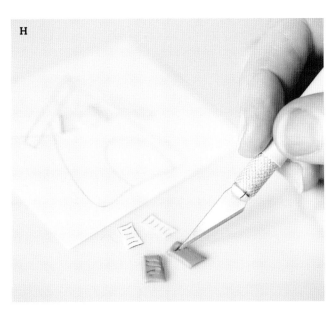

3 Take the no. 18 piping tube and, using the smaller end as a cutter, carefully cut and remove the window. Replace with a circle of the same size cut from very thinly rolled navy paste.

4 Cut the roof from dark orange modelling paste and attach in place. Finally, cut the shutters from thinly rolled light orange modelling paste. Add lines to each shutter using a craft knife, being careful not to cut all the way through the paste **(H)**. Attach in place. Roll some of the trimmings into a small ball and attach as a door knob.

> Small things have a way of
> overmastering the great.
>
> Sonya Levien

Adding the trees and sky

1 Roll out half of the green paste between 2mm (1/16in) spacers, or barbecue skewers, and half between 1mm (1/32in) spacers. Using the suggested circle cutters and both ends of the no.18 piping tube, cut out circles from the pastes. Make at least one circle 4.3cm (1¾in) in diameter for the tallest tree. Use the 2mm (1/16in) thick paste for the largest paste ring of each tree and the 1mm (1/32in) thick paste for the inner rings. Leave the cut-out circles of paste for the trees on your work surface to firm up a little, and to help prevent the circles distorting when lifted.

2 Create trees of differing sizes on your work surface by stacking the cut circles in size order **(J)**, ensuring that they are placed centrally. Attach the trees to the cake, using sugar glue, with the large tree to the side of the house standing proud of the top of the cake.

3 For the tree trunks, roll out the navy modelling paste between the 2mm spacers and by using a craft knife and straight edge cut out 2mm (1/16in) to 5mm (¼in) wide strips of paste. Attach a strip of a suitable width to each tree as a trunk and trim to fit.

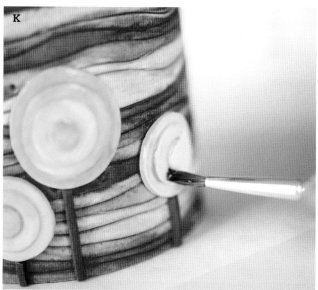

4 To complete the trees, dilute a selection of green paste colour in cooled boiled water or clear alcohol and paint over the rings of paste to exaggerate and highlight **(K)**.

5 Finally, roll out the remaining navy paste between 1mm (1/32in) spacers and cut out an 8mm (3/8in) wide strip. Paint sugar glue around the top edge of the covered cake. Then starting at one side of the tallest tree, wrap this navy strip around the top edge of the cake giving it the feeling of movement by allowing it to undulate up and down fractionally from the horizontal, as shown **(L)**. Cut the strip to fit using the 4.3cm (1¾in) circle cutter, as used for the tallest tree.

Let's go fly a kite!

Studying Hundertwasser's painted landscapes made me think of flying kites with my children, high up on the top of the Chiltern Hills with the rolling countryside beneath us. So I have created a sugar kite variation to the main cake.

You will need

* ✳ **cake:** 7.5cm (3in) round
* ✳ **sugarpaste (rolled fondant), modelling paste and paste colours:** as for the main cake, plus a little black modelling paste
* ✳ dab of navy blue royal icing
* ✳ **cake board:** round hardboard, same size as your cake
* ✳ 1mm (1/32in) spacers (LC)
* ✳ kite template
* ✳ cutting wheel
* ✳ no.1 PME piping tube
* ✳ sugar shaper
* ✳ template
* ✳ craft knife

1 Roll out the pink modelling paste between 1mm (1/32in) spacers. Place the kite template on the pink paste and cleanly cut around the edges of the template using a craft knife. Allow to dry thoroughly.

2 Cover and paint the mini cake, as for the main cake and add the band of dark blue sky as before.

3 Roll out small amounts of pale green, dark orange and red modelling paste between the 1mm (1/32in) spacers, and cut out 2cm (3/4in) long 3mm (1/8in) wide strips from each colour. Fold the ends of each strip into the middle to form a bow. Attach the kite to the cake using a dab of navy blue royal icing, and support in place whilst the icing dries. Once dry attach the bows in place.

4 To create the string, soften some of the black modelling paste so it is really quite soft. Do this by first kneading in some white vegetable fat and then dunking the paste into cooled boiled water and re-kneading. Repeat until it feels soft and stretchy. Place the paste together with a no. 1 PME piping tube into the sugar shaper. Squeeze out two lengths of paste from the sugar shaper onto your work surface, one short one long. Then take a paintbrush and attach them to the kite, as shown on the finished cake.

5 Finally, add some green tassels to the kite as shown using the sugar shaper and the pale green modelling paste.

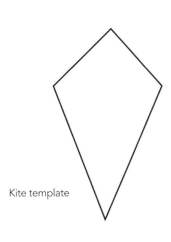

Kite template

63

White Wedding

Today, most of us associate the colour white with weddings, but it has not always been so. Queen Victoria is credited with starting the current tradition by wearing an off-white satin gown decorated with ornate handmade lace for her wedding in 1840. This was considered a rather unusual choice at the time as it was more customary to wear coloured gowns. After Queen Victoria's wedding, wearing white was quickly copied by wealthy, fashionable brides, but it was not fully adopted until after the second world war, influenced in part by the wedding attire depicted in Hollywood blockbusters and an increase in prosperity.

Pretty damson blossom, the perfect backdrop for a spring wedding

Morning dew drops on a delicate white Camellia Japonica flower

Creating the White Wedding Cake

Weddings are very special days, so I have created a couple of very special contemporary white cakes. The main centrepiece cake is topped with sugar roses, leaves and blossoms together with moulded white sugar hearts, while the simpler variation cake is topped with a large heart. The sides of each cake are decorated with white fringe swags made with a sugar shaper. Make one to give as a gift or simply take elements and decorate a cake for every guest.

You will need

MATERIALS
* **cake:** 6.5cm (2.5in) round mini cakes
* **sugarpaste (rolled fondant):** white
* buttercream
* **modelling paste:** white
* **flower paste:** white
* sugar glue
* snowflake edible lustre dust
* white nonpareils

EQUIPMENT
* **cake board:** 6.5cm (2.5in) round hardboard, the same size as your cakes
* **cutters:** Lindy's large flat floral cutter (LC), rose leaf cutter set (FMM), 3cm (1¼in) five-petal flower cutter (PME), Lindy's pointed oval cutters (LC)
* block of polysterene
* 5mm (¼in) spacers (LC)
* scriber (PME)
* cocktail sticks (toothpicks)
* ball tool
* sugar shaper
* no.1.5 PME piping tube (PME)
* double-sided rose leaf veiner (GI)
* flower formers (optional)
* heart mould set (AM)
* foam pad with cut out holes (PME)
* stay fresh mat
* soft dusting brush
* paintbrush
* dressmakers' pin
* palette knife

See Suppliers for list of abbreviations.

Rose cones

1 Make these in advance so they can dry thoroughly. Roll a ball of white modelling paste in your hand then place your forefinger partially on top of the ball, roll the ball backwards and forwards until the ball turns into a cone.

Tip
The cone should be the same length as the width of the petals on the large flat floral cutter.

2 Insert a cocktail stick (toothpick) into the base of the cone **(A)** and place into the block of polystyrene or covered oasis. Repeat. Leave the cones to dry out completely.

A

Covering the cake and adding the fringe swags

1 Level your mini cake to a height equal to the diameter of the cakes. If you baked your cake in multi-mini tins then this height will be the top edge of the tin. Attach the cake to a hardboard cake board the same size as the diameter of the cake using buttercream as glue.

2 Cover the cake with buttercream and white sugarpaste, referring to the instructions in the Basics section.

3 Make a paper circle template the same size as the top of your cake. Fold the circle in half three times and unfold, your circle should be divided into eight equal sections. Place the template on top of the cake, securing with a dressmakers' pin. Use a scriber to mark the position of each fold line around the outside of the circle **(B)**.

4 To make fringes, soften some of the modelling paste so it is very soft. Do this by firstly kneading in some white vegetable fat and then dunking the paste into cooled boiled water and re-kneading. Repeat until it feels really soft and stretchy.

5 Place the paste together with the no. 1.5 piping tube into the sugar shaper. Squeeze out 15cm (6in) and 20cm (8in) lengths of paste onto your work surface **(C)** – if the paste doesn't come out easily it isn't soft. You will need about 28 of the shorter lengths and 24 of the longer ones, but I suggest you make a few extra to allow for breakages. Leave the lengths to firm up on your work surface so they can be handled easily without breaking.

6 Paint sugar glue over the top of the covered cake. Take one of the longer lengths and place one end over one of the scribed marks, drape the length down the side of the cake so it hangs 3cm (1¼in) from the base of the cake. Then place the second end on the next-but-one mark, in other words a quarter of the way around the top of the cake.

7 Add five more lengths **(D)** to make the swag, making each length slightly shorter and allowing a couple of lengths to cross over as shown.

> We cannot all do great things, but we can do small things with great love.
>
> Mother Teresa of Calcutta

B
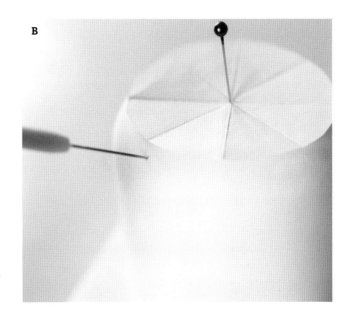

C

D
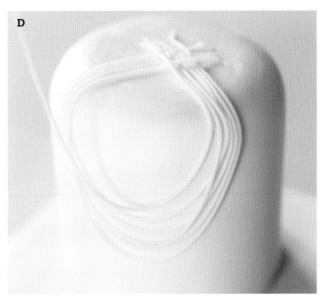

8 Repeat for the fringe swag opposite the first. Then add the ones on either side, placing the ends of the fringes on top of the first two. Add the remaining four swags in the same way using the shorter lengths **(E)**. Position this top layer of swags so they overlap the first layer, again using the scribed lines to help with positioning **(F)**.

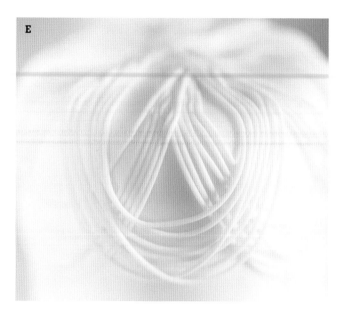

Making the hearts

1 Knead a small amount of modelling paste to warm it, then roll a 1.5cm (⅝in) ball of paste. Place the paste into the 1.5cm (⅝in) high heart mould ensuring that the sugar surface being placed into the mould is perfectly smooth. Push the paste into the mould firmly. Then stroke the paste around the edges of the mould with your finger to help it fill the mould completely **(G)**.

Tip
It's important that the surface of the sugar that you push into the mould is absolutely smooth. If there are small joins they will probably be visible on your finished piece.

2 Remove any excess paste with a palette knife so the back of the mould is flat. To remove the paste, carefully flex the mould to release.

Creating the roses

Make one open rose and one half rose following the instructions below:

1 Very thinly roll out the white flower paste. Cut out a five-petal shape using the large flat floral cutter, turn it over and place it on a foam pad. Take the ball tool and stroke around the edges of each petal by pressing the tool half on the petal and half on the pad to soften the cut edge and to frill slightly **(H)**.

Tip
To make these petals the paste should be almost transparent, so you can see your work board through it.

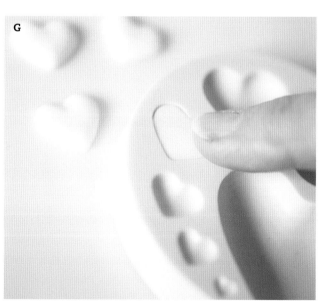

H

I

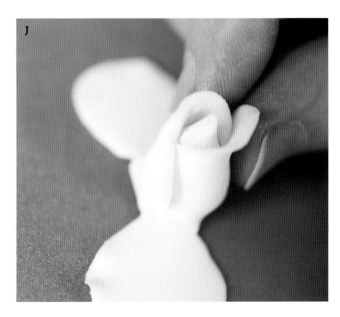

J

K

2 Turn the paste back over and place the centre of the blossom over one of the holes in the foam pad. Cover one of the petals (petal 1) with sugar glue and insert a rose cone on a cocktail stick through the centre of the blossom. Take the glued petal and wrap it tightly around the cone to create a spiral, making sure that the centre of the bud is not visible **(I)**.

3 Working anticlockwise, half cover petals 3 and 5 with sugar glue. Then wrap petal 3 around the cone making sure it stays open at the top. Tuck one edge of petal 5 under petal 3, then wrap petal 5 around the cone **(J)**. Finally, half cover petals 2 and 4 with glue and wrap them around the other petals on the cone **(K)**.

4 Cut out and soften the edges of the second layer of petals in the same way as for the first layer, then paint a line of glue along one side of each petal and in the centre.

5 Place the cocktail stick through the centre of the paste as before and turn the whole flower upside down, arrange the petals so they overlap each other and stick in place. Allow the petals to harden slightly before turning upright, allow the petals to open a fraction.

6 For the third layer of petals, soften the edges of the petals as before then using a cocktail stick, roll back two edges of each petal at an angle to the middle **(L)**.

7 Turn the paste over and cup the centre of each petal with the ball tool. Lightly paint the base of each petal with glue, then insert a half rose through the centre and turn the whole flower upside down, allow the petals to fall into a natural position and stick them in place. Leave the flower for a few minutes then turn it upright, allowing the petals to fall open slightly – if you turn the flower too early the outer layer will not be firm enough and will flop down the stem.

Creating the leaves

Make approximately six rose leaves in various sizes and eight to ten small leaves, as follows:

1 Thinly roll out some white flower paste or firm modelling paste and cut out leaves using the rose leaf and smaller pointed oval cutters. Place under a stay fresh mat or a sheet of clear plastic until they are required to prevent drying out.

2 Place a few leaves on a foam pad. Take the ball tool and stroke around the edges of the paste by pressing the tool half on the paste and half on the pad to soften the cut edge.

3 Next place a leaf in the double-sided veiner, press down hard on the top of the veiner and then release, and remove the veined leaf **(M)**. You will be able to see at this point if your original paste was the correct thickness, if the leaf looks a bit fleshy then the paste was too thick, if the leaf has fallen apart in the veiner then the paste was probably too thin.

4 Place veined leaves onto dimpled foam, formers or scrunched up paper towel and allow to dry partially in a natural shape.

Creating the blossoms

1 Thinly roll out some white modelling paste and cut out three blossoms using the five-petal flower cutter. Place your petals on to a foam pad. Then take the ball tool, place it in the centre of a petal, stroke towards the centre of the flower pressing on the tool as you do so, to cup the petal. Repeat for the remaining petals and flowers.

2 To enable each flower to retain its cupped shape, place it in a former, if you have one, and allow to partially dry.

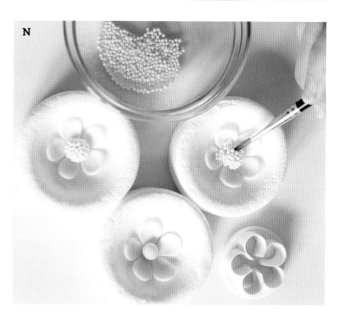

O

Tip

Ready-made polystyrene formers in a number of sizes are available, but you can easily make your own using tin foil cupped over the top of a circle cutter, a cup, glass or other object with a circular rim.

3 For the flower centres, roll three small balls of modelling paste. Place in the centre of each flower and coat with sugar glue. Pour a few nonpareils on top of the glued balls, leave for a moment or two then tip the flowers upside down to remove the excess. Take a paintbrush and adjust the positioning of the nonpareils so that the flower centres are completely coated **(N)**. Attach in place.

Adding the decoration

1 Use some of the sugarpaste trimmings to create a small dome. Place this onto the top of the cake and cover with sugar glue. It should still be possible at this stage to remove the cocktail sticks in the roses by carefully twisting them. Next take the partially dry flowers, leaves and moulded hearts and arrange as desired **(O)**, referring to the photograph of the finished cake for guidance.

2 To add a touch of romance and glamour, apply a delicate sparkling sheen of edible lustre dust over the floral decoration using a soft dusting brush.

Heart-topped cake

I have decorated this simpler cake using three of the same techniques as the main cake, to give you ideas as to what else is possible. For the heart I have used the largest heart in the mould set and decorated it with nonpareils. Once you have experimented with these techniques yourself I'm sure you'll feel confident to adapt and change my designs to create your very own.

MILESTONES

71

Teddy Surprise

Teddy bears are always a childhood favourite: teddies loved until they are threadbare, teddies in all shapes and sizes from tiny ones on key rings to ones that have to be hugged with adult-sized arms. From teddies with soft plush fur that's asking to be stroked to valuable antique bears with pointed snouts and upright ears, most of us at one time or another have had a very special bear that has a place in our hearts, one we will always remember. This irresistible little bear could be customized to match a favourite teddy, and the colours and patterns decorating his sugar and cake gift box can be changed to suit whatever scheme you have in mind.

Handmade and much loved bear showing his age with replacement paw pads and wonky eyes

This cute adorable teddy is everyone's friend!

My daughter's trusted companion who went everywhere with us when she was a little girl

Creating the Teddy Surprise Cake

This adorable sugar bear is propped up neatly inside its sugar cake box, a perfect gift for a teddy lover. The side panels are made individually and simply stuck together to surround the box cake, so it can easily be personalized for any occasion.

You will need

MATERIALS
* **cake:** 6.5cm (2 ½in) chocolate cube
* **sugarpaste (rolled fondant):** white and brown
* chocolate ganache
* **modelling paste:** brown, white, violet, peach, red, dark pink, light pink, light brown and very dark brown
* pastillage
* sugar glue
* royal icing to stick the lid together

EQUIPMENT
* **cake:** square hardboard, the same size as your cake
* waxed paper
* foam pad
* smoothers x 2
* **spacers:** 1mm (1⁄32in) and 5mm ¼in) (both LC)
* ball tool
* Dresden tool
* craft knife
* ruler
* stay fresh mat
* sugar shaper with small mesh and small square discs
* palette knife

See Suppliers for list of abbreviations.

Covering the cake

1 Level your mini cake to a height equal to the width and length of the cake to create a cube. Place the cake on the hardboard cake board the same size as the cake.

2 Next cover your cake in a couple of layers of chocolate ganache using the techniques described in the Basics section. Make sure all the corners are sharp and the ganache has set before moving on to the next step.

Tip
I used a firm chocolate cake and ganache here so that the cake would be able to support the weight of the teddy. Another alternative would be to use fruitcake and a layer of marzipan.

3 Knead the white sugarpaste to warm it and then roll it out using 5mm (¼in) spacers. Carefully pick up the paste and place it onto waxed paper flipping the sugarpaste over, so the underside is uppermost.

4 Place the cake on its side onto the sugarpaste and using a palette knife, cut away the excess paste, ensuring that the palette knife is flush with the cake to achieve a straight cut **(A)**. Repeat for the remaining three sides, and lastly the top.

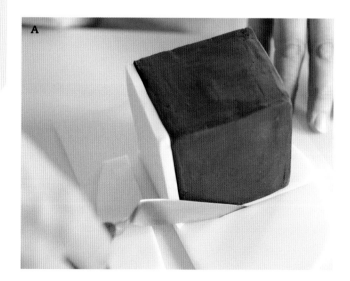

A

5 Place the cake upright on its base and, using smoothers, adjust the soft sugarpaste covering to ensure all sides are perfectly smooth and vertical and all edges are sharply upright **(B)**.

Tip

Smoothers are the best tools to help you achieve flat sides with sharp edges.

Making the box sides and lid

1 Measure the sides of your cake and cut out rectangular paper templates to fit each side accurately, adding 1.5cm (⅝in) to the height to allow for the lip of the box. Measure the top of your cake and cut out a square paper template 6mm (¼in) larger than the top for the lid. Cut out templates for the sides of the lid, the same length as the top and 2cm (¾in) deep.

2 Roll out the pastillage between 1mm (¹⁄₃₂in) spacers and, using your templates and a craft knife, cut out four box sides, one lid and four lid sides **(C)**. Lift each piece carefully, ensuring that its shape does not distort, and place on a foam pad to dry thoroughly.

Tip

Drying the pastillage in an airing cupboard is ideal if you have one, or alternatively a warm oven that has been swtiched off – you are aiming to remove the moisture from the paste.

3 Once the pastillage is completely dry you can, if necessary, file any rough edges away using an emery board or fine sand paper.

Decorating the box sections

1 Knead all the colours of modelling paste to warm them, adding a little white fat and water if the paste is a bit dry and crumbly. You want the paste to be pliable but firm. Individually roll out each of the colours between 1mm (¹⁄₃₂in) spacers. Using spacers to do this means that each stripe will be the same thickness, so the finished pattern will look smooth and uniform.

2 Take a ruler and craft knife and cut strips of varying widths from each colour **(D)**. Leave the paste on your work surface to firm up for a few moments before covering with plastic or a stay fresh mat to prevent the icing drying out further.

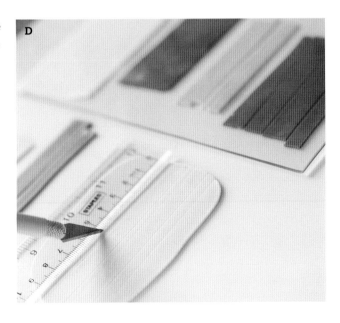

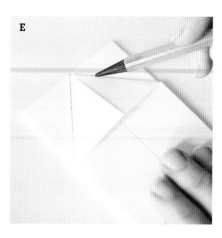

E

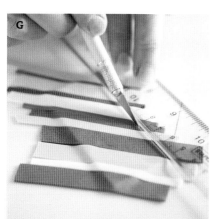

F

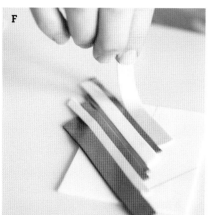

G

3 Take one of the dried pastillage side pieces. Add placement guidelines as follows: take a pencil and draw a vertical line to divide the tallest side in half. Next take a paper side template, fold in half lengthways then fold in the two adjacent top corners to meet the central fold. Place the template on the pastillage side and draw along these two folds as shown **(E)**. This will allow you to place your paste with accuracy to create the abstract chevron design.

4 Paint sugar glue over one half of the pastillage side. Using the cut modelling paste strips place onto the glue, using the placement lines to guide you. Change the colour and width of each strip as you go **(F)**.

5 Cut the central vertical join in the pattern straight by using a craft knife and ruler **(G)**, double check you have cut this in the correct place by referring to the marked line. Turn the side over onto a clean work surface and using a craft knife cut the excess paste away cleanly **(H)**, you will achieve a sharper cleaner finish by cutting it this way. Turn back over and adjust, if necessary, using a smoother.

6 For the second half of the side pattern, place your folded template under a stay fresh mat and use as a guide to mitre one end of each strip before adding to the second side as shown **(I)**. Fill the side with strips as before and flip to cut away the excess. Repeat for the remaining three sides. Attach the completed sides to the covered cake, making sure they are all square and true.

7 For the corners and top trim, soften some of the peach modelling paste so it is really quite soft. Do this by first kneading in some white vegetable fat and then dunking the paste into cooled boiled water and re-kneading. Repeat until it feels soft and stretchy. Place the paste together with the small square disc into the sugar shaper. Squeeze out eight lengths of paste from the sugar shaper **(J)** and leave on your work surface to firm up a fraction.

H

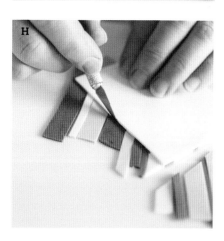

I

J

8 Paint a little sugar glue into the vertical gap at each corner and along the rim of the box. Insert a peach length into each corner cutting flush with the top of the box. Add the peach top trim, cutting to fit at each corner. Allow to dry.

9 Decorate the lid as for the box sides, but this time the pattern is split into four sections. Once complete, cover each lid side with light pink modelling paste. Then use royal icing to securely attach the sides to the lid. Place to one side to dry.

Making the teddy

1 Using the brown sugarpaste, roll a 6cm (2⅜in) wide ball and cut in half. Place one half at an angle inside the box to create the visible part of the teddy's body.

2 Roll a 1.5cm (⅝in) wide sausage and cut into two 5cm (2in) lengths. Round and flatten one end of each to create the paws and cut the other ends at an angle of 45 degrees. Attach to the bear's body, positioning the arms so they rest on or over the sides of the box.

3 For the head roll a 4cm (1½in) ball of paste, flatten the ball in the palm of your hand to make the head wider and thinner, then press down on the ball to reduce its height. Attach to the body with sugar glue, so the widest section becomes the face. The elements of the bear's body are shown below **(K)**.

4 For the ears, roll a 2cm (¾in) ball of paste and cut in half. Shape the ears by inserting a ball tool as shown **(L)**. Attach each ear in place on either side of the head.

Tip
To make your cake really special, colour your paste to match a beloved bear.

K

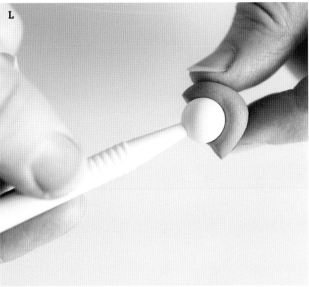

L

N

5 For the snout, roll a 2.5cm (1in) ball of light brown modelling paste, cut in half and place one half on the face of the bear. Mark the mouth with a cutting wheel. Take the dark brown modelling paste and roll two small balls for eyes and model a triangular nose. Attach in place with sugar glue.

6 Soften some of the brown modelling paste so it is really quite soft (see Decorating the box sections). Place the paste together with the smallest mesh disc into the sugar shaper. Squeeze out a short tuft of paste and remove with the sharper end of a Dresden tool **(N)**. Add the tuft to the teddy's body for fur. Continue adding tufts until you have completely covered the body, arms and head of the teddy **(O)** but leave the eyes and snout visible.

7 Finally, add a sugar bow under the teddy's chin. Make the bow by cutting a 7mm (⅜in) wide by 7cm (2¾in) long strip from thinly rolled red modelling paste. Bring both ends into the centre of the strip and pinch to secure and gather slightly **(P)**. Wrap another short strip over the join to represent the knot.

O

P

Teddy gift boxes

Create small contemporary box cakes using the colours from the main cake. This is an excellent opportunity to experiment with patterns made from cut out pastes. Top each box with a charming cut-out teddy.

You will need

* **cake:** 5cm (2in) cubes
* **sugarpaste (rolled fondant), modelling paste and paste colours:** as for the main cake
* sugar glue
* **cake board:** square hardboard, same size as your cake
* **spacers:** 1mm (¹⁄₃₂in) and 5mm (¼in)
* craft knife
* ruler
* stay fresh mat
* **cutters:** small circle cutter and teddy from teddy bears picnic cutter set (PC)

1 Cover the boxes with sugarpaste as for the main cake. Decorate the sides of each box using vertical strips, or cut-out half circles. Add 1.2cm (½in) wide strips of modelling paste to the top of each side to create the lid. Finally add a square of modelling paste to each decorated cake to create the top of the box lid.

2 Very thinly roll out the brown paste – the thickness of paste is critical here, too thick and the shapes will not cut out cleanly, too thin and the embossed detail will not be as prominent. Take the teddy bear cutter and press the head firmly into the rolled out paste.

3 Remove the excess paste. Cut out a snout from thinly rolled light brown paste and attach on top of the cut out teddy head. Add a flattened ball of dark brown paste for a nose. Carefully lift the completed head and attach centrally to the top of a lid. Repeat for the remaining boxes.

Tip

Leave the rolled out paste
on your work surface
to firm up slightly before
using, as this helps ensure
that the paste doesn't
stick inside the cutter.

Bottled with Love

What could be sweeter than a contented, gurgling baby after he has had his fill of milk? Infancy is such a fleeting and special time. Nights can sometimes feel very long but a well-fed bouncing baby with their waving arm gestures and babbling sounds delights us all. Like human babies young polar bear cubs also grow on a rich diet of milk and their playful antics are cute and endearing, which I think makes them a very suitable decoration for a baby bottle cake. You can, of course, change the bottle colours so the cake is more suitable for a little girl. In the shops you will find bottles in a multitude of shapes, sizes and colours. I have used a simple bottle shape but if you are feeling adventurous why not carve your cake into a more interesting ergonomic bottle!

Pastel colours and a simple repeated decoration on a patterned baby's bottle

Examples of different bottle teats — the shapes can vary slightly

Creating the Polar Bear Bottle Cake

This baby bottle cake is simply created by stacking two mini cakes. The polar bear decoration is made by using a simple cutter, and the teat is modelled by hand from modelling paste. The cake would make an excellent baby shower present or a cake to welcome a new arrival.

CHILDHOOD

You will need

MATERIALS
* **cake:** two 5cm (2in) round mini cakes
* **sugarpaste (rolled fondant):** ice blue, golden brown and white
* buttercream
* **modelling paste:** white, golden brown, turquoise, dark teal and black
* sugar glue

EQUIPMENT
* **cake board:** 3.5cm (1⅜in) round hardboard or cake card (you may need to trim a larger board down to fit)
* **spacers:** 1mm (¹⁄₃₂in) and 5mm (¼in) (both LC)
* scriber
* ruler and set square
* carving knife
* craft knife
* teat template
* **cutters:** polar bear (PC), 4.3cm (1¾in), 3.6cm (1⅜in), 3cm (1⅛in) circles, and Lindy's scalloped diamond (LC)
* sugar shaper
* teat template

See Suppliers for list of abbreviations.

Covering the cake

1 Level your mini cakes to a height equal to the diameter of the cakes. If you baked your cake in multi-mini tins then this height will be the top edge of the tin. Spread buttercream over the top surface of one cake and stack the second on top, then place the stacked cakes in the freezer. Once frozen, remove from the freezer and immediately, using a carving knife together with a set square, adjust the sides of the cake to make them all perfectly vertical **(A)**. To curve the top and bottom edges of the cake, take a pair of scissors and carefully cut small sections of cake away. You can use a knife to do this but scissors will ensure that only small uniform amounts of cake are removed **(B)**.

2 Using buttercream, attach the cake board to the base of the cake. Carefully cover the sides and top of the cake with a thin layer of buttercream to act as glue for the sugarpaste.

3 Knead 220g (7⅞oz) of ice blue sugarpaste to warm it and then roll it out using 5mm (¼in) spacers. Turn the paste over and cut into a 13cm (5in) wide strip. Place the cake on its side on this paste, aligning the base of the cake with one edge. Roll up the cake in the paste **(C)**, using a smoother as a guide. Where the two sides of the sugarpaste meet, trim the paste to create a neat join and rub closed using the heat of your fingers. The join will be easily disguised by the decoration.

4 Stand the cake upright and fold the sugarpaste over the top of the cake to give a smooth curved finish to the top edge of the bottle. Using scissors cut away the excess paste from the centre and flatten to give a horizontal finish with a smoother. Don't worry about the appearance as this area will be covered with the teat, just make sure it's level. Leave to dry, ideally overnight.

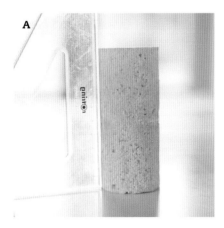

A

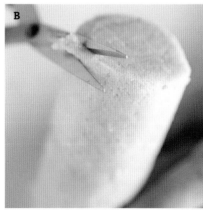

B

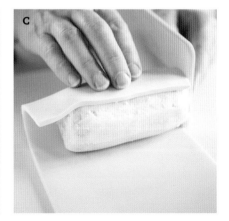

C

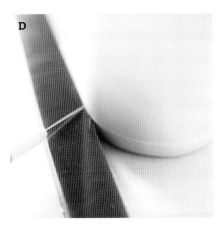

Adding the decoration

1 Stack your 5mm (¼in) spacers and place up against your cake. Take a scriber and mark a 1cm (½in) placement line all the way around the cake **(D)**. Next, using your set square, scribe a placement line around your cake at a height of 9.5cm (3¾in) above the base. Finally, scribe two vertical lines opposite each other between the two scribed rings.

2 Knead the turquoise and dark teal modelling pastes to warm, adding a little white fat and cooled boiled water if the paste is a little dry and crumbly, you want the paste to be pliable but firm. Individually, roll out the modelling pastes into at least 20cm (8½in) long strips, using 1mm (½2in) spacers. Take a ruler and craft knife and cut out two 3mm (⅛in) wide lengths from each paste **(E)**. Leave the paste on your work surface to firm up for a few moments.

3 Paint a line of glue above the 1cm (½in) scribed ring and below the 9.5cm (3¾in) scribed ring. Pick up a dark teal strip and place carefully on top of one of the glued lines, cutting it to fit with a craft knife. Adjust the positioning as necessary so that the strip looks horizontal. Add the second teal strip to the second glued line and then add the turquoise strips above and below, as shown on the main photograph of the cake.

4 Paint a thin line of glue over each scribed vertical line. Soften some of the golden brown modelling paste with extra white vegetable fat and cooled boiled water, so it is really quite soft. Place the paste together with the small round disc into the sugar shaper. Squeeze out two lengths of paste from the sugar shaper and leave on your work surface to firm up a little before positioning vertically over the glued line. Cut each length to size using a craft knife **(F)**.

5 For the volume marks on the bottle, roll out some white modelling paste between 1mm (½2in) spacers and, using the smallest scallop diamond cutter, cut out seven shapes. Attach these at equal intervals up the side of the bottle as shown **(G)**.

6 To add the polar bear, begin by kneading the white modelling paste to warm it. Very thinly roll out the paste. The thickness of paste is critical here, too thick and the shapes will not cut out cleanly, too thin and the embossed detail will not be as prominent. Take the polar bear cutter and press it firmly into the rolled out paste.

Tip
To make your white paste a brilliant white knead
in a little super-white dusting powder.

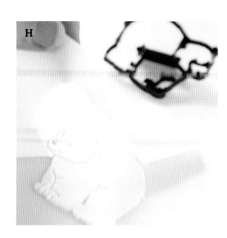

7 Remove the excess paste from around the outside of the cut-out shape. Then, with the help of a scriber or similar tool, remove the paste from between the front and back legs **(H)**. If you are struggling to get a clean cut around the edges, take a craft knife and carefully cut around the shape to neaten. Attach in position on the cake using sugar glue, then add a small black ball for a nose.

Adding the bottle screw ring and teat

1 For the screw ring, roll out the golden brown sugarpaste to 1cm (½in) thickness. Take the 4.3cm (1¾in) and 3.6cm (1⅜in) circle cutters and cut out one circle with each. Stack the paste circles and smooth the uppermost cut edges with a finger **(I)**.

Tip
Use two sets of 5mm (¼in) spacers to help give
your paste a 1cm (½in) uniform thickness.

2 For the base of the teat, roll out some white sugarpaste between 5mm (¼in) spacers and cut out a 3cm (1¼in) circle using the appropriate cutter. Place on top of the golden brown sugarpaste screw ring and smooth the top edge with a finger to curve the paste.

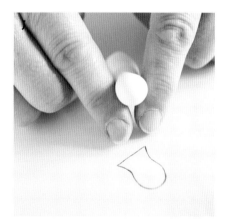

3 For the teat, roll a 1.5cm (⅝in) wide sausage of white sugarpaste then, using the template below to guide you, thin the teat by rolling the sausage backwards and forwards between your fingers **(J)**. Cut the teat to size then pinch around the base to shape **(K)**. Once you are happy with the overall shape, attach in place. Finally, lift and place the screw ring and teat in position onto the cake, securing in place with sugar glue.

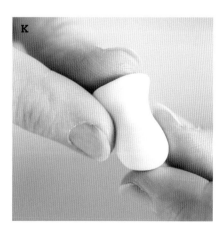

Teat template

CHILDHOOD

Pink bottle

For this cake I've changed the bottle colour so it's more in keeping with the colours parents traditionally choose for little girls, and swapped the polar bear for embossed circles of butterflies, bears and bees.

You will need

* **cakes:** two 5cm (2in) round mini cakes
* **sugarpaste (rolled fondant):** pale pink, beige and white
* buttercream
* **modelling paste:** in six different colours
* sugar glue
* equipment as for the main cake, plus:
* **cutters:** 1.6cm (⅝in) circle cutter (use wide end of a PME piping tube), and plunger blossom cutter (PME)
* **embossers:** bee embosser from Countryside Borders Autumn Set 7 (HP), butterfly embosser from Daisy Chains and Butterflies Set 18 (HP), and teddy embosser from Toytime Set 16 (HP)

1 Construct and cover this bottle as for the main cake. Add a pink strip, as for the main cake.

2 To make the decoration, cut small circles from thinly rolled out modelling paste and emboss some with suitable embossers. Add these circles in rows to the covered bottle cake using sugar glue, experimenting with placement and colours. You can add more or less decoration, it's entirely up to you but don't be afraid to experiment to get the effect you want.

3 Model the screw ring and teat as for the main cake and secure in place with sugar glue.

> When you work on the little things big things happen.
>
> Roger Halston

Rainbow Love

W ho can fail to be delighted at the sight of a rainbow, with its kaleidoscope of shimmering colours, from the inner arc of cool blues out to the warm reds? I'm sure most of us were too young to remember when we saw our first rainbow, but my guess is that we were all picked up and shown it as soon as one appeared. Rainbows are a fascinating natural phenomena, even if the pot of gold at the end remains elusive! Interestingly, in literature, a rainbow is often used as a metaphor for hope and happiness, so I think it makes a very lovely theme for a children's cake. Simply adapt my design to suit the child in question by changing the hair colour, skin tone and nappy design.

My son, always a cheeky 'monster'!

What a look! Inquisitive happy babies are always a delight

Stylized mixed-up rainbow design on the cover of a note pad

Creating the Rainbow Love Cake

For this rainbow-inspired mini cake, I have created love hearts in each of the main colours of the rainbow and used them together with rainbow stripes to add fun and colour. Children love to see themselves portrayed on cakes so this modelled sugar toddler, which can easily be personalized, makes this a wonderful first birthday cake. I guarantee everyone will know who's on top!

You will need

MATERIALS
* **cake:** 7.5cm (3in) round mini cake
* **sugarpaste (rolled fondant):** white
* buttercream
* **modelling paste:** flesh, black, pink, purple, blue, green, yellow, orange and red
* **edible dust:** rose pink
* **sugar glue**
* **paste colour:** black

EQUIPMENT
* **cake board:** round hardboard, the same size as your cake
* toddler template
* plastic sleeve
* **spacers:** 1mm (1/32in) and 5mm (1/4in) (both LC)
* Dresden tool
* ball tool
* craft knife
* small scissors
* **cutters:** seven concentric circle pastry cutters no bigger than 6.5cm (2½in), and Lindy's elegant heart cutter set (LC)
* round piping tubes no.18 and 3 (PME)
* stay fresh mat
* cocktail sticks (toothpicks)
* polystyrene block or cake dummy on which to build the model
* paintbrush
* palette knife

See Suppliers for list of abbreviations.

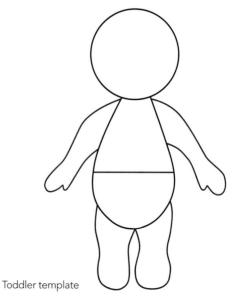

Toddler template

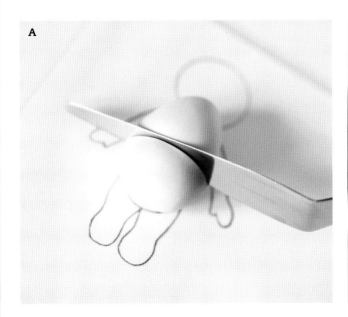

A

B

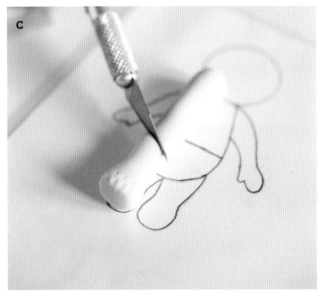

C

Modelling the toddler

1 Photocopy the template and place in a plastic sleeve.

2 Knead the blue modelling paste to warm it, adding a little white fat and water if the paste is a little dry and crumbly, you want the paste to be pliable but firm.

3 Roll the paste into a 3cm (1¼in) wide ball. Elongate one side of the ball by rolling it backwards and forwards between your fingers to create a rounded cone that fits the template. Place the blue cone on the template and, using a palette knife, cut in half along the nappy line, as indicated on the template **(A)**. Keep the wider lower half. Repeat, using a ball of flesh coloured paste, but this time keep the more pointed upper half. Stick the two retained halves together using sugar glue.

4 Roll out a strip of blue modelling paste, using 1mm (⅟₃₂in) spacers. Then using a ruler and craft knife, cut out a 2mm (⅟₁₆in) wide ribbon and attach around the top of the blue nappy to disguise the join.

5 For the legs, roll a tapered sausage to roughly fit the template. Shape the ankle by rolling and thinning the paste between your fingers. Form the foot by squeezing the paste to form the toes. Using a craft knife, make four small cuts to form five toes **(B)** and mark nails by indenting each toe with a Dresden tool. Place the leg back on the template and cut the top of the leg to fit **(C)**. Repeat for the second leg.

6 Take two short cocktail sticks (toothpicks) and, using a twisting motion, insert one up through each leg so that they project by approximately 2cm (¾in) below the foot and 1cm (½in) above the leg. Glue the legs to the body **(D)** and insert the legs vertically in to the polystyrene so that the toddler stands vertically. Insert another cocktail stick into the body to later support the head.

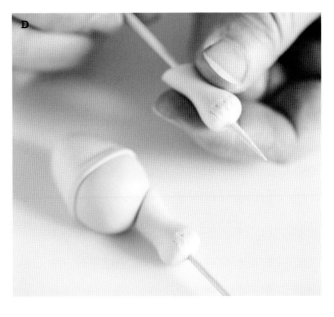

D

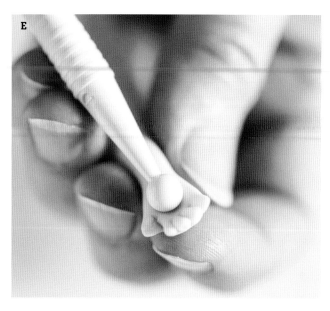

E

F

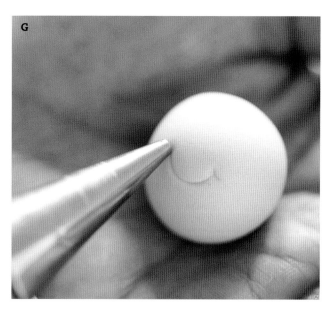

G

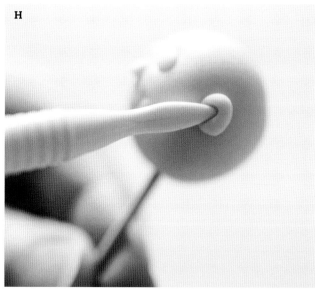

H

7 For the arms, roll a tapered sausage of flesh coloured modelling paste to fit the template. Roll and thin the paste to shape the wrist. Flatten the hand and, with a pair of small scissors cut out a small triangle to form the thumb. Cut the fingers and gently roll each to shape then mark the fingernails with the tip of a Dresden tool. Cup the hand slightly with a ball tool **(E)**.

8 Place the arms on the template again and cut to the required length, ensuring that the hand is in the correct position before making the angular cut. Attach in place with sugar glue and position as desired, supporting the arms as necessary whilst they dry and firm up **(F)**.

9 For the head, roll a 2.5cm (1in) ball of flesh coloured modelling paste. For the smile, hold a no.18 piping tube at 45 degrees and indent the mouth, add corners to the smile using a no.3 tube **(G)**. Indent eye sockets with the small end of a ball tool and add a small pinched ball of paste for a nose. Insert a cocktail stick into the base of the head and leave to dry thoroughly.

10 Roll two small balls of white paste and insert into the eye sockets. For the ears take two small balls of paste and stick them to the sides of the head. To shape the ears press the broader end of a Dresden tool onto the centre of the ball and drag it carefully sideways so the edge of the ball is blended into the face, and the remaining paste forms a 'C' shape **(H)**.

11 Dilute some black paste colour and using a fine paintbrush paint the eyes leaving a small white light spot **(I)**. Gently dust some edible pink dust over each of the toddler's cheeks. Roll a short tapered sausage of black modelling paste, curl it and attach to the top of the head for hair.

12 For the neck, add a small tapered sausage around the cocktail stick on the torso, see the photograph for guidance **(J)**. Attach the head in place on the neck and adjust to give the toddler the most pleasing expression.

Covering and decorating the cake

1 Level your mini cake to a height equal to the diameter of the cakes. If you baked your cake in multi-mini tins then this height will be the top edge of the tin. Attach the cake to a hardboard cake board the same size as the diameter of the cake using buttercream as glue.

2 Cover the cake with buttercream and sugarpaste, referring to the instructions in the Basics section. Once you are happy with the finish, place the cake to one side to dry.

3 Roll out the pink modelling paste into a 30cm (12in) long strip, using 1mm (1⁄32in) spacers. Take a ruler and craft knife and cut out a 2mm (1⁄16in) wide pink ribbon **(K)**. Leave the paste on your work surface to firm up for a few moments.

Tip
Using spacers when you roll out your paste will ensure that each band of the rainbow will be the same thickness, so the finished rainbow will look uniform.

> Don't be afraid to give your best to what seemingly are small jobs. If you do the little jobs well, the big ones will tend to take care of themselves.
>
> Dale Carnegie

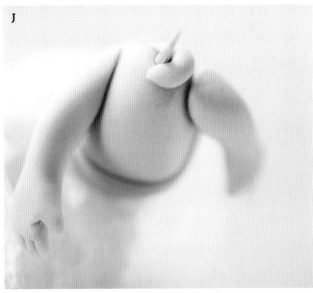

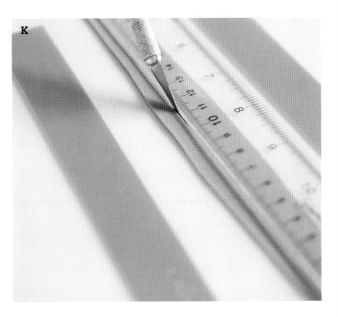

4 Paint a line of glue around the base of your covered cake. Pick up the pink strip and wrap it carefully around the base of the cake, cutting it to fit with a craft knife. Repeat for the remaining colours of the rainbow, ensuring that you add each colour in the correct order: pink, purple, blue, green, yellow, orange, red. Also make sure that the strips neatly abut each other as you place them, if necessary use a palette knife to help ease them into position **(L)**.

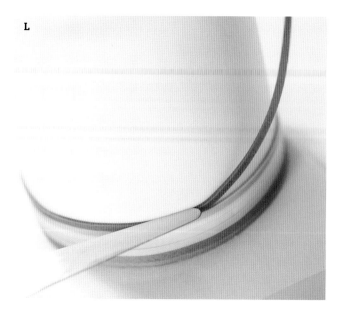

5 Next, individually roll out each of the rainbow modelling paste colours, between 1mm (⅟₃₂in) spacers, and cover with plastic or a stay fresh mat to prevent the icing drying out. Cut out at least four hearts from each colour, using the middle (2.8cm [1⅛in] high) cutter from the elegant heart set. Allow the hearts to firm up on your work surface. Then, using sugar glue and a paintbrush, attach the hearts in order around the sides of the cake as shown **(M)**. You may need to adjust the positioning of the hearts slightly to allow them all to fit neatly around the cake.

6 Using the 6.5cm (2½in) circle cutter, cut a circle from the rolled out red paste. Leave the circle where it was cut, this prevents the circle distorting, and carefully remove the excess paste. Take the slightly smaller circle cutter and centrally remove a circle from the larger circle. Replace this circle with an orange one and blend the join between the two circles by rubbing a finger over the pastes so there is no gap between them. Continue removing and replacing circles of different colours until your rainbow is complete **(N)**.

Tip
A scriber is an excellent tool to help remove
the cut circles that are not required.

7 Lift the completed rainbow carefully from your work board using a palette knife, and attach centrally to the top of your mini cake.

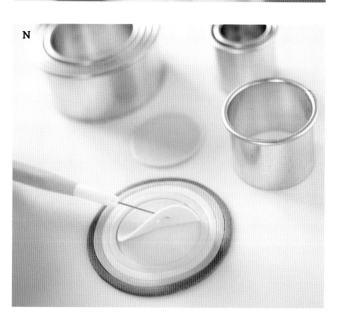

8 Finally, to add the toddler, carefully remove the dried sugar model from the polystyrene and position on top of the cake, the cocktail sticks in the legs will help to ensure that he stands securely. Note that the model should be removed from the cake before cutting because it contains inedible and potentially sharp cocktail sticks.

Bunches of balloons

Young children love balloons, so I've added them to the sides of these mini birthday cakes in rainbow-coloured bunches. Just add a number or name to the top of each cake to personalize it.

You will need

* **cakes:** 5cm (2in) round, covered in white sugarpaste
* **modelling paste:** as for the main cake
* sugar glue
* 1mm (1/32in) spacers (LC)
* **cutter:** small petal from Lindy's Viola Leaf and Petal Cutter Set (LC)
* Dresden tool
* cutting wheel
* no.1 PME piping tube
* sugar shaper
* paintbrush

1 Roll out the green modelling paste into a long strip. Use a ruler and craft knife to cut out 5mm (¼in) wide strips, one for each cake. Create textured grass by running a cutting wheel repeatedly over one side of each strip. Attach one textured strip to the base of each cake, encouraging movement in the textured grass.

2 Cut out rainbow-coloured balloon shapes from thinly rolled modelling paste using the viola petal cutter. Texture the tied end of each balloon by pressing the sharper end of a Dresden tool into the paste a few times. Once the balloons are partially dry, attach them in groups to the sides of the cakes.

3 To create the strings, soften some of the black modelling paste so it is really quite soft. Place the paste together with a no. 1 PME piping tube into the sugar shaper. Squeeze out lengths of paste from the sugar shaper onto your work surface, then take a paintbrush and attach them to the balloons, as shown on the finished cakes.

4 To personalize the cakes add sugar or candle numbers.

Autumn Magic

The fleeting, transient and beautiful colours of the natural world in autumn make this time of year particularly fascinating to me. Colours explode on the trees all around us like fireworks, whilst the landscape is bathed in golden sunlight, making everyday drab colours look much more appealing and spectacular. It's also at this time of year that toadstools and fungi suddenly appear, as if by magic! Going on fungi forays into the woods is always exciting, you never know what you will find. The child in me wants to look for fairies, whilst the artist in me is delighted by seeing fungi in attractive sculptural forms and groupings.

A stately ink cap with its signature black edge

Bracket fungi with rippling edges

Beech masts scattered in the leaf litter

Autumnal sycamore leaf backlit by golden sunlight

Creating the Autumn Magic Cake

For my autumnal mini cake, I have taken the smokey blue skies of autumn as a backdrop and decorated the cake itself with cut-out sugar fungi, which I have painted to give a more realistic look. I have added grass and soil to place the fungi in a natural setting. Perfect for someone who, like me, is fascinated by nature. The cake can easily be personalized by adding a sugar number or name to the top.

You will need

MATERIALS
* **cake:** 6.5cm (2.5in) round mini cake
* **sugarpaste (rolled fondant):** smokey blue
* buttercream
* **modelling paste:** white, deep cream, light green, mid green, dark green and light brown
* **paste colours for painting:** selection of browns and greens plus black
* super white dusting powder
* sugar glue
* clear alcohol, e.g. gin or vodka (optional)

EQUIPMENT
* **cake board:** round hardboard, the same size as your cake
* craft knife
* stay fresh mat
* ruler
* ball tool
* **cutters:** fungi cutters from the Fairies set (PC), Lindy's curled leaf cutters (LC), and Lindy's flame cutters (LC)
* foam pad
* 1mm (¹⁄₃₂in) spacers (LC)
* paintbrushes
* paint palette

See Suppliers for list of abbreviations.

Covering the cake

1 Level your mini cake to a height equal to the diameter of the cakes. If you baked your cake in multi-mini tins then this height will be the top edge of the tin. Attach the cake to a hardboard cake board the same size as the diameter of the cakes using buttercream as glue.

2 Cover the cake with buttercream and then the smokey sky blue sugarpaste, referring to the instructions in the Basics section. Once you are happy with the finish, place the cake to one side to dry.

> Love of beauty is taste.
> The creation of beauty is art.
>
> Ralph Waldo Emerson

Decorating the cakes

1 Knead the deep cream modelling paste to warm it, adding a little white fat and cooled, boiled water if the paste is a little dry and crumbly. You want the paste to be pliable but firm. Very thinly roll out the paste. The thickness of paste is critical here, too thick and the shapes will not cut out cleanly, too thin and the embossed detail will not be as prominent.

Tip

Leave the rolled out paste on your work surface to firm up slightly before using, as this helps ensure that the paste doesn't stick inside the cutters.

2 Take the two different-sized mushroom cutters from the fairies cutter/embosser set and press them firmly one by one into the rolled out paste as shown **(A)**. You will need approximately three or four of each, depending on how you wish to arrange them on the cake. Using a craft knife, cut away the grass from the base of the mushroom as shown **(B)**.

3 Very thinly roll out the white modelling paste and cut out about five shaggy ink caps. Place the cut out shapes under a stay fresh mat or plastic bag to prevent them drying out.

Tip

If you are struggling to get a clean cut around the edges of the fungi, take a craft knife and carefully cut around each shape to neaten.

4 Measure the diameter of your cake: the easiest way to do this is to wrap a piece of string or ribbon around your cake and measure the length. The diameter of a covered 6.5cm (2½in) cake is approx 23cm (9in). Place your ruler on your work surface, imagine the ruler is the base of the cake, and position the cut out mushrooms and ink caps along the ruler from zero to 23cm (9in), or the diameter of your cake. Vary the heights, groupings and angles of the fungi, and allow them to overlap with each other to give a natural appearance **(C)**.

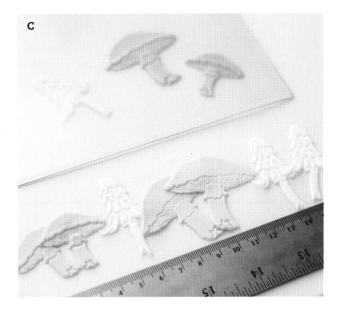

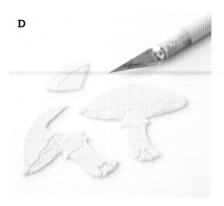

D

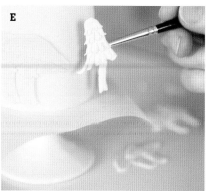

E

5 Where the fungi overlap, use a craft knife to cut away all but a margin of the paste that lies underneath. This allows the uppermost mushrooms and ink caps to retain their smooth uniform appearance but gives the fungi on the cake a slight three dimensional appearance **(D)**. Using sugar glue and a brush attach the fungi to the cake **(E)**.

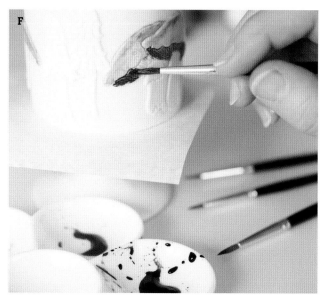

F

Painting the fungi

1 In a paint palette, mix a selection of edible paste colours with cooled boiled water or clear alcohol to create suitable colours to paint with. Select an appropriate brush and apply a golden brown colour wash to the caps of the mushrooms and a dark brown wash to their gills **(F)**. Make sure that the wash fills the embossed lines to really help the gills look lifelike. Mix some of the super white dust into the diluted golden brown, crushing the grains of powder to make a smooth paint. Use this to paint the mushroom stalks. Paint the annulus or ring at the top of the stalk white.

2 For the ink caps apply a brown wash over each cap ensuring the paint sinks into the embossed markings. Take a dry flat headed brush and remove most of the brown wash, as shown **(G)**. Allow to dry.

G

3 Next add a second layer of painted detail to each of the fungi. For the mushrooms, use a fairly dry brush and stipple darker and lighter colours over sections **(H)**.

4 For the ink caps add a touch of golden brown to the tips and stems of each, then add the characteristic black ink to the lower edges of each cap. With your brush carefully blend the black into the brown of the lower cap so there is no harsh line **(I)**. Allow to dry.

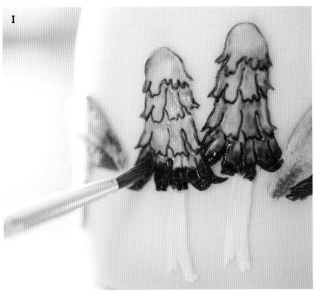

"The small things people do and say mean more to me than big ones. Small things seem more sincere."

MJ Christine

J

The soil and grass

1 Roll out the light brown modelling paste and tear it into thin uneven strips with your hands to give the paste a jagged edge, attach around the base of the cake in sections using sugar glue. Take your Dresden tool and using the more pointed end, create the soil texture by pushing and pulling the tool through the paste (**J**).

2 Thinly roll out the three green modelling pastes between 1mm (1/32in) spacers. Cut out blades of grass from each colour, using suitable cutters from the curled leaf and flame cutter sets (**K**). Store under a stay fresh mat to prevent drying out.

3 To curl some of the blades, place on a foam pad and using a ball tool stroke from the tip of a blade down the shape, the amount of pressure you exert will determine how much the grass curls (**L**). Also experiment by placing the ball half on the paste and half on the pad. Once you are happy with the shapes pinch the lower edges of each blade together as shown (**M**).

4 Attach the grass to the cake, cutting some to fit, using a craft knife or a fungi cutter. The idea is that the taller blades appear as if behind the fungi whilst the shorter ones are positioned in front. Once dry, paint over the grass with diluted green paste colours, and the soil dark brown.

> " From a small seed a mighty
> trunk may grow. "
>
> Aeschylus

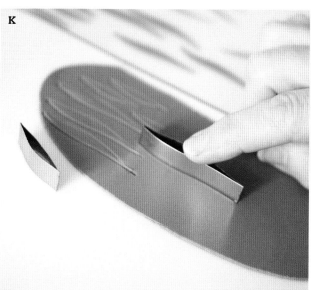

K

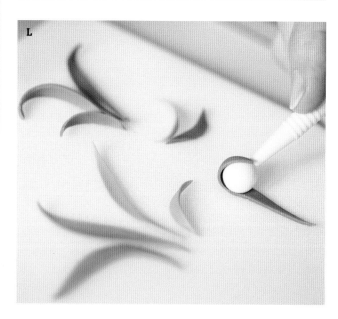

L

M

Nature's fireworks

I couldn't resist decorating this cake with a couple of trees in all their autumn glory. Halloween comes right at the end of autumn, so why not add a pumpkin or two a the foot of the trees, and give as a special trick or treat gift?

You will need

* **cake:** 6.5cm (2.5in) round mini cakes
* **sugarpaste (rolled fondant):** smokey blue
* **modelling paste:** light brown, dark brown, red, orange, yellow and pale green
* **paste colours:** brown, red, orange, yellow and green
* **cake board:** round hardboard, the same size as your cakes
* **cutters:** Lindy's pointed oval cutters (LC), mole cutter from the teddy bear's picnic set (PC)
* double sided leaf veiner
* foam pad
* ball tool
* Dresden tool
* pumpkin mould from garden mould set (AM) (optional)

1 Thinly roll out the modelling pastes and cut out leaves using the small pointed oval cutters and place on a foam pad. Take your ball tool and stroke around the edges of each leaf by pressing the tool half on the paste and half on the pad to soften the cut edge.

2 Next, place a leaf in an appropriate double sided veiner, press down hard on the top of the veiner and then release and remove the veined leaf. If the leaf looks a bit fleshy then the paste is too thick, if the leaf has fallen apart in the veiner then the paste is probably too thin. Once you are happy, pinch the base of the leaf together and repeat for the remaining leaves.

3 Using the dark brown modelling paste model the trunk and lower branches of two trees on your work board. Add bark texture by stroking your Dresden tool through the soft paste. Once you are happy with the size and shape of each trunk, attach one either side of the cake using sugar glue.

4 Position each leaf onto the cake to create the intertwining canopy, encouraging movement in the paste to give a more natural look to the leaves.

5 Add soil as for the main cake. Finally, hand model or use a mould to create a small pumpkin or two to sit at the base of the tree, and add a cut-out mole using the suggested cutter.

Passion for Paisley

As long ago as I can remember I have been fascinated by the intricate patterns and rich colours of Southern Asia. This is partly, I think, because I grew up on tales of colonial India from a hundred years ago, passed down through my family. Even as a child I remember being shown complex, carved, three-dimensional trinkets and delicately embroidered fabrics. These memories, together with my own visits to this rich and diverse continent have subsequently influenced my work. Of all the patterns used in Indian decorative art, it is the curled droplet shape of paisley that I find the most attractive. Gold and silver paisley shapes are often woven into beautiful silks for weddings and other special occasions so it seems highly appropriate to create paisley shaped celebration cakes too.

The rich colours used in this fabric are enticing – especially the gorgeous red!

Decorative paisley patterns on a woven woollen shawl

Metallic thread gives this embroidery an opulent shimmer

A modern take on a paisley pattern creates a decorative edge to this headscarf

Creating the Passion for Paisley Cakes

To decorate these individual paisley cakes I have taken the intricate art of paper quilling and created decorations to reflect traditional Asian flower and scroll embellishment. These sumptuous cakes would make a fabulous birthday present for someone special or amazing wedding favours for an Asian bride.

You will need

MATERIALS
* **cake:** from which to cut paisley shapes, e.g. for one shape 12 x 8cm (4¾ x 3¼in) rectangle; for two shapes 12cm (4¾in) square; for eight shapes 24cm (9½in) square.
* **sugarpaste (rolled fondant):** red and purple
* buttercream
* **modelling paste:** purple, plum, red, pink, dark cream, brown
* sugar glue

EQUIPMENT
* paisley template
* **cake board:** hardboard, cut into paisley shapes the same size as your cakes
* 1mm (⅟₃₂in) spacers (LC)
* ruler
* craft knife
* cocktail sticks (toothpicks)
* stay fresh mat
* small scissors

See Suppliers for list of abbreviations.

Carving and covering the cakes

1 Level the cake to a height of 3.5cm (1⅜in). Photocopy the paisley template (see below) and make a paper template for each cake you plan to carve and decorate. Place the templates on your cake, using cocktail sticks (toothpicks) to secure. With a sharp knife, cut vertically through the cake around the edge of each template **(A)**. Remove the templates and place your cake in a freezer.

Tip
Once you have cut out your outline shape, turn the cake over so the base shape has a cleaner cut.

∂e℮o⋅2ℓℓ

2 Once frozen, remove from the freezer and carve as follows: to shape the wider end of a paisley, carve in a gentle curve from the centre of the cake down to all the lower edges **(B)**.

3 To shape a tail, carefully cut from the centre of the cake down towards the tip of the tail **(C)**. Gently curve and round all remaining edges. Then repeat for the remaining cakes.

4 Attach the cakes to a hardboard cake board using buttercream as glue. Cover the cakes with buttercream and then red or purple sugarpaste, referring to the instructions in the Basics section. Once you are happy with the finish, place the cake to one side to dry.

A

B

C

Quilling

1 Knead the purple modelling paste to warm it, adding a little white fat and cooled boiled water if the paste is a little dry and crumbly, you want the paste to be pliable but firm. Roll out the paste into a long strip, using 1mm (1/32in) spacers so that the paste is of a uniform thickness. Cut one edge straight using a ruler and craft knife. Place the ruler at right angles to the cut and mark the paste at 3mm (1/8in) intervals using a craft knife, as shown **(D)**.

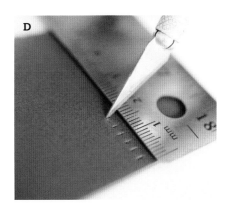

2 Then, using these marks, cut out 3mm (1/8in) wide strips **(E)**, and leave on your work surface to firm up slightly, before covering with a stay fresh mat or plastic. Repeat for the other modelling paste colours.

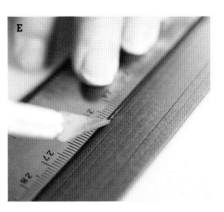

3 To create the two tone red/pink strips, separately roll out the red and pink pastes between 1mm spacers (1/32in), place the rolled out red paste on top of the pink paste and re-roll between the spacers to reduce the thickness. Mark and cut 3mm (1/8in) strips as for the single colour strips. Once you have a supply of paste strips you are ready to start quilling.

4 Most shapes in quilling are made by rolling strips, in this case of modelling paste, and then pinching them into a shape. I suggest you make the elements of the design as follows, before attaching them to your cake.

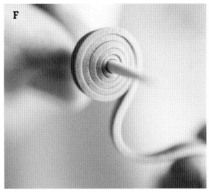

Tight coils: Pick up one end of a brown strip and gently press onto the tip of a cocktail stick (toothpick). Roll the cocktail stick until you have six circled layers of paste around the stick **(F)**. Carefully slip the paste coil from the stick and cut away the excess paste. Secure the cut end of the strip to the coil using a damp paintbrush. Make ten three-layered tight pink coils, fourteen two-layered dark cream tight coils and seven four-layered tight purple coils. Cut the purple coils in half and if necessary, stick the sections together using a dab of water.

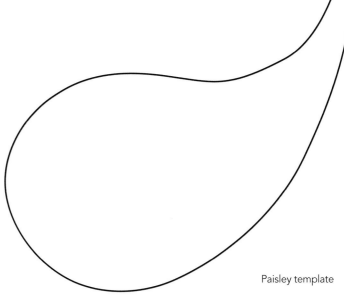

> For the person for whom
> small things do not exist,
> the great is not great.

Jose Ortega y Gasset

Paisley template

G

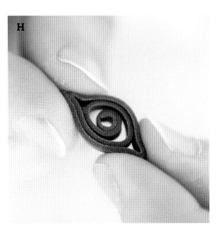

H

I

J

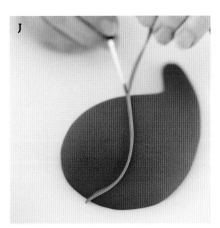

K

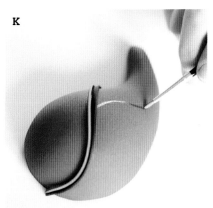

Loose coils: Using red modelling paste strips, make two tight coils but do not cut or secure their ends. Place on your work surface and with the help of a cocktail stick carefully unwind and loosen the coils **(G)**. Once you are happy with the shapes, leave on your work surface to firm up. Make approximately fifteen loose plum coils in differing sizes, and two pink ones. Leave to firm.

Marquise or eye: Make three loose plum coils, cut away the excess and fix the ends to the coils with a dab of glue. Next, carefully pinch either side of the coils to make the characteristic marquise or eye shape **(H)**. Then make two small black marquises.

Teardrop: I have slightly adapted the technique here to make it a little easier when working with sugar. Using the two-tone red-pink paste, with the pink side innermost, fold a strip over to make a small teardrop shape. Press the paste together at the tip of the teardrop with your fingers. Next, add another layer around the first, leaving space between the layers. Cut away the excess paste then pinch to shape and secure **(I)**. Add a third layer, then place to one side. Make a matching two-tone teardrop. Then create a four-layered red teardrop and a two-layered long brown teardrop.

Decorating the red paisley cake

1 Paint a curved 's' shaped line of glue from the top of the covered cake to a point midway down the inside of the shape and attach a brown strip on its thinnest edge as shown **(J)**. Referring to the main cake as reference, add a further black strip to one side of the brown strip. Next, paint a curved glue line from the middle of the 's' to the opposite side of the cake, as shown **(K)**. Attach a black strip on top and cut to size. Attach all the tight coils to the cake with the exception of the dark brown coil, which is added in step 2 to the flower.

2 Create the flower shape on your work board using the elements already created **(L)**. Once you are happy, attach in position on your cake. Create a purple base to your flower by first making a loose coil and then pinching it on three sides to create a triangle shape. Attach in place and add the long brown teardrop as a stem.

3 Add the purple and pink scrolls to the cake referring to the main cake and step for guidance **(M)**, cutting each scroll stem to size as appropriate. Finally, add the large red teardrop and two small black marquises.

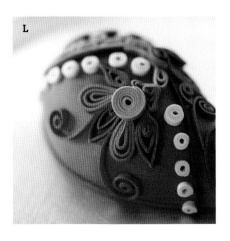

Purple Paisley

Using the same colour palette but a different colour balance, I have decorated this slightly simpler paisley cake using exactly the same method. Once you have experimented with these techniques yourself I'm sure you'll feel confident to adapt and change my designs to create your very own.

Marvellous Marigolds

Every year self-sown marigolds, or *calendula* to give them their Latin name, brighten up my garden with wonderful splashes of bright yellows, golds and oranges. What could be more cheerful! These easy-to-grow flowers bloom brightly all summer long and well into the autumn and mild winters. On sunny days I like to sit and watch the butterflies and bees flying from one flower to another feasting on the nectar – it's a mesmerizing sight. If you've never tried growing flowers, these colourful calendula are a good variety to start with even if you don't have a garden as they also grow really well in pots in a sunny spot.

A beautiful bright orange marigold, a vibrant example of a calendula variety

The dark centre of this marigold is very eye-catching against its yellow petals

Creating the Marvellous Marigold Cakes

I used to make a lot of sugar flowers when I had more spare time, but I still occasionally like to sit and pull a real flower apart and then reconstruct it in sugar. For these mini cakes I have taken the calendula flowers in my garden and done just that. For the side decoration I have created a simple design, taking inspiration from the two leaf seedling form that seems to spring up all over my flower beds.

DESIGNER

You will need

MATERIALS
* **cake:** 5cm (2in) round mini cakes
* **sugarpaste:** ivory
* buttercream
* **modelling paste:** brown, light orange, green and light green
* orange flower paste
* sugar glue
* **edible dust:** dark orange and burgundy
* royal icing, small amount to attach the flowers in place

EQUIPMENT
* **cake board:** round hardboard, the same size as your cakes
* **spacers:** 1mm (1/32in) and 5mm (1/4in) spacers (both LC)
* cutting wheel
* **cutters:** Lindy's calendula cutters (LC), Lindy's small teardrop cutter set (LC) and Strawberry calyx
* stay fresh mat
* 3mm (1/8in) perfect pearl mould – BR130 (FI)
* daisy centre stamp (JEM)
* double-sided small rose leaf veiner (GI)
* double-sided lily petal veiner (GI)
* flower formers (optional)
* plain paper
* sticky tape
* paintbrush
* palette knife

See Suppliers for list of abbreviations.

Creating the marigolds

1 The marigolds can easily be made in advance and allowed to dry in paper cones, which will hold the flowers' shape. To make the paper cones, cut out 7cm (2¾in) or larger circles from white paper. Take one circle and fold into quarters and unfold, where the folds meet should be the centre of the circle. Use this circle to mark the centre of the other circles.

2 Next, take a pair of scissors and make one cut into the centre of each circle. Take the two cut edges and overlap them by about 2.5cm (1in) to create a shallow cone, securing them together with sticky tape **(A)**. Support the cones in flower formers, round pastry cutters or other suitable objects, such as glass jars **(B)**.

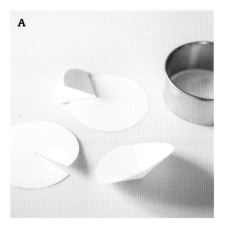

A

B

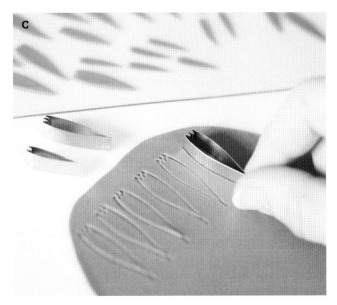

C

3 To create the petals, thinly roll out the orange flower paste. Using the calendula cutter set, for each flower cut out approximately 20 of the largest petal, 15 of the middle-sized petal and a few smaller petals **(C)**.

Tip
Store your freshly cut petals under
a stay fresh mat so they don't dry out.

4 Working in batches, place a few of the larger petals on a foam pad and stroke around the cut edges with a ball tool, holding the tool so it is half on the paste and half on the pad **(D)**. This helps to thin the edges of the petals and removes the sharply cut edge.

5 Taking one petal at a time, place it on top of one half of a double-sided veiner and cover with the second half making sure the veiner is lined up correctly. Press firmly down onto the top of the veiner to emboss the paste petal. Release the petal **(E)** and place to one side. Repeat the same process for all the remaining cut out petals.

6 Using the longest petals, create the outer layer of the flower by placing between 10 and 12 petals into one of the paper cone formers as shown **(F)**, leaving a small gap between the tips of each petal.

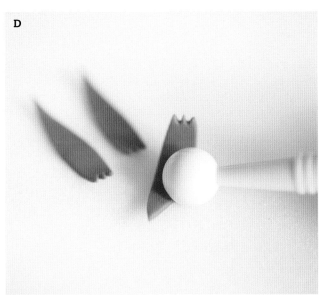

D

" Simple pleasures are best. "

Alan Bradley

E

F

7 Add a second layer, positioning the petal between the first. Use small pieces of twisted kitchen paper to prop the petals up away from the first layer **(G)**. This also helps to give the petals movement and make them look more lifelike. Add the third layer using the middle-sized petals and finally add a few of the smaller petals. Adjust the position of the petals to look lifelike, using twisted paper as required.

8 To create the flower centres, roll a ball of brown modelling paste and press it firmly into the daisy centre stamp, you want just enough paste to fill the mould without spilling out over the edges. The moulded sugar should come away cleanly from the mould attached to your finger. Make one for each flower and attach in place.

9 Roll out the brown modelling paste into a long strip. Use a ruler and craft knife to cut out 5mm wide strips, two for each flower. Texture the edge of each strip by running a cutting wheel repeatedly over one side **(H)**. Roll and cut an orange strip of paste. Using the end of one of the cutters remove small triangles of paste to create a serrated edge all along one side of the strip **(I)**.

10 Stack these strips with the orange one in the middle like a sandwich, so that small thin triangles of orange are clearly visible. Press the strips together then, using a craft knife and straight edge, remove any surplus paste from the back of the stack **(J)**.

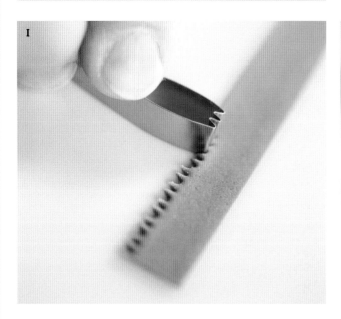

DESIGNER

11 Wrap the sandwiched strip around the outside edge of the moulded flower centre and cut to fit. Using a Dresden tool, add movement to the layers of paste so that the circles do not look so uniform. Once you are happy with the centre and the placement of the petals, dust the outer edge of all the petals with the suggested dust then allow the flowers to dry thoroughly.

12 Thinly roll out some green modelling paste and cut out calyces using the strawberry calyx cutter, two for each marigold. Take a craft knife and cut each sepal in half lengthways. Place on a foam pad and elongate and thin the sepals. Do this by stroking a ball tool from the centre of the calyx to the tip of each sepal **(K)**. Finally, attach the calyx to the dried backs of each flower, using two layers per marigold.

Covering and decorating the cake

1 Level your mini cake to a height equal to the diameter of the cakes. If you baked your cake in multi-mini tins then this height will be the top edge of the tin. Attach the cake to a hardboard cake board the same size as the diameter of the cake, using buttercream as glue. Cover the cake with buttercream and ivory sugarpaste, referring to the instructions in the section.

2 Take a cutting wheel and mark vertical stems at varying heights into the sides of the cakes at intervals **(L)**. Refer to the photograph of the completed cake for guidance. Once you are happy with the finish, place the cake to one side to dry.

K

L

Think big thoughts but
relish small pleasures.

H. Jackson Brown, Jr.

DESIGNER

3 Separately roll out the light orange, green and light green modelling pastes, using 1mm (¹⁄₃₂in) spacers. Using the two smallest cutters from the teardrop set, cut a selection of leaves from the different colours. Using the double-sided rose leaf veiner, vein all the darker green leaves, positioning the paste in the veiner so the widest part of the leaf is nearest the top of the veiner **(M)**.

4 Attach the leaves in pairs to the top of each indented stem, using sugar glue. Try to position the leaves so they do not overlap and vary the leaf colour from seedling to seedling as you go around the cake.

5 For the soil, knead the brown modelling paste to warm, and roll into a thin long sausage. Place on top of the 3mm (⅛in) section of the perfect pearl mould, press the paste into the mould first with your fingers and then the back of a Dresden tool. Using a palette knife, cut away the excess paste and then release the pearls by flexing the mould along its length, so the pearls fall out without breaking or distorting **(N)**. Allow the pearls to firm up a little before attaching them around the base of your cakes using sugar glue.

6 Finally, place a dab of royal icing on the back of each marigold and attach one to the centre of each cake.

M

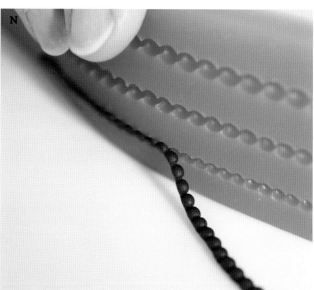

N

Tip

Use firm modelling paste to make the brown pearls, if your paste is too soft the string will break easily.

White chrysanthemum

To simplify the decoration and save a lot of time, I have used a beautiful detailed mould to create the flower for this bridal white cake.

You will need

* ✳ **cake:** 5cm (2in) round, covered in white sugarpaste
* ✳ white modelling paste
* ✳ sugar glue
* ✳ 1mm (⅟₃₂in) spacers (LC)
* ✳ cutting wheel
* ✳ **cutters:** Lindy's small teardrop cutter set (LC)
* ✳ **moulds:** 3mm perfect pearl mould – BR130 (FI) and chrysanthemum mould – FL270 (FI)

1 Cover and decorate the cake as for the main project but use white pastes.

2 To create the chrysanthemum, roll a small amount of modelling paste into a ball and press into the centre of the mould. Then take a larger ball of paste and place on top of the first ball ensuring that the sugar surface being placed into the mould is perfectly smooth. If there are small joins visible they will probably be visible on your flower. Push the paste into the mould firmly to ensure the deeper sections of the mould are filled. Then stroke the paste around the edges with your finger to help it fill the mould completely.

3 Remove the excess paste with a palette knife but leave a slight dome on the back of the mould, otherwise the flower will not remain complete when de-moulded. Remove the flower from the mould by carefully flexing the mould all the way around until it releases. Attach the flower to the top of the cake.

Time for Tinsel

At Christmas time we all love to see trees decorated with twinkling lights, colourful baubles and sparkling stars. It's all part of the fun and festivities. My tree at home always has a colour theme, but amongst the baubles and tinsel there are decorations that I have collected throughout the years from my travels; wooden dolphins from New Zealand, hand-painted Santas on elephants from India, jangling penguins from Australia and intricate laser-cut nutcracker shapes from Germany. Each year hanging this eclectic mix of decorations, together with the angels and stars made a long while ago by my children, is a special moment, a moment that transports me back to other places and other times… I love it!

Sparkling detail on a hairband, so very Christmassy

A stunning stylized Art Deco dove, that belonged to my grandparents

Embroidered felt box with a starburst design — my very own handiwork!

Creating the Time for Tinsel Trees

For these festive mini cakes, I have carved each cake into a cone to represent the traditional shape of a Norway spruce tree. The cakes are then given a modern twist. I have used a theme of birds and snowflakes, but you can, of course, select your own decorative shapes and colour scheme. Why not try small angels, candy canes or stars? Or for a more jazzy Christmas, choose deep rich reds and oranges to give a sense of warmth and sumptuousness.

You will need

MATERIALS
* **cake:** two 5cm (2in) round mini cakes for each tree (choose a firm dense cake), ideally baked in multi mini tins
* **sugarpaste (rolled fondant):** dark brown, deep blue-green and white
* buttercream
* **modelling paste:** white, dark blue-green, aqua and pale mid-green
* snowflake edible lustre dust
* sugar glue
* white royal icing

EQUIPMENT
* **cake board:** round hardboard, the same size as your cakes, one per tree
* 18mm (¾in) wide wooden dowelling or similar for the trunk
* cocktail stick
* **cutters:** dove from the Christmas midi set (PC), small bird from Make a Cradle cutter set (PC), 2.5cm (1in) Snowflake plunger cutter (PME), Lindy's eight flat-ended petal flower from flat floral collection set one (LC), Lindy's eight petal pointed petal flower from flat floral collection set one (LC), 2cm (¾in) daisy marguerite plunger cutter (PME), and circle cutter – use a no.18 piping tube (PME)
* sugar shaper and small round disc
* **spacers:** 5mm (¼in) and 1mm (¹⁄₃₂in) (both LC)
* dusting brush and paintbrush
* no.1.5 PME piping tube
* piping bag
* palette knife or craft knife

See Suppliers for list of abbreviations.

Making the tree trunks

1 These can be made in advance and stored until needed. Take the wooden dowelling and, using an appropriate saw, cut into 2.5cm (1in) lengths. You will need one for each tree you are planning to make. Check that your cuts are completely straight and discard or re-cut any that are not. This is important because you don't want your finished tree to look as if it's about to topple over!

2 Knead the dark brown sugarpaste to warm it and then roll it out using 5mm (¼in) spacers. Turn the paste over and cut it into 2.5cm (1in) wide strips, one for each tree trunk. Paint sugar glue over the sides of your cut dowels. Place each onto a paste strip and roll up **(A)**. Cut the strips to create neat straight joins and rub closed using the heat of a finger.

3 Stand the trunks upright on waxed paper and check the fit of the sugarpaste, adjust as necessary. Place to one side to dry.

Tip
You could add bark texture to the trunk using modelling tools or embossers.

Carving the cakes

1 Level all the cakes to a height of 5cm (2in), if you baked your cake in multi-mini tins then this height will be the top edge of the tin. Spread buttercream over the top of half the cakes and stack the others on top. Attach the base of each cake to the hardboard cake board again using buttercream as glue. Place your stacked cakes in a freezer until frozen.

2 Make a paper circle template the same size as your cakes. Fold the circle into quarters and then unfold. Where the folds meet should be the centre of your circle. Working on one cake at a time, place the template on top of a set of stacked frozen cakes. Then partially insert a cocktail stick through the centre of the template **(B)**.

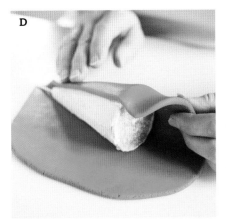

3 Carefully remove the template, leaving the cocktail stick in place. Position the cake on its side and using a sharp knife cut from the cocktail stick to the cake board all the way around the cake to create a cone shape **(C)**. Once you have the basic shape, place the cake upright and stand back from it to check that your cone is symmetrical. Adjust as necessary. Once you are happy with the shape, repeat for the remaining cakes. Cover each cake with foil or plastic to prevent it drying out.

Tip
If you have a small gap between your cake and the outside edge of the board, fill it with a few cake crumbs.

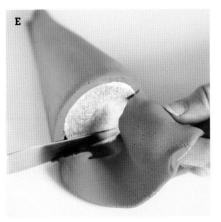

Covering the green tree

1 Take one of the carved cakes and carefully cover with a thin layer of buttercream to act as glue for the sugarpaste. Knead the dark blue-green sugarpaste to warm it and then roll it out using 5mm (¼in) spacers. Turn the paste over and cut one edge straight. Place the cake on its side on this cut edge. Roll up the cake in the paste **(D)**. Note that as the cake is cone shaped, you will find that the cake rolls in an arc, so make an allowance for this when positioning the cake on the sugarpaste.

2 Where the two sides of the sugarpaste meet, trim the paste to create a neat join and rub closed using the heat of your fingers – note the join is easily disguised by the decoration. Next take a palette knife and, holding it flush with the cake board on the base of the cake, cut away the excess sugarpaste **(E)**.

3 Attach the covered cake centrally to a prepared trunk using royal icing as glue. Cover your remaining cakes and ideally place to one side to allow the sugarpaste to crust over.

Decorating the cake

The doves

1 Next make the doves. Knead the white modelling paste to warm it, adding a little white fat and water if the paste is a little dry and crumbly – you want the paste to be pliable but firm. Very thinly roll out the paste, the thickness is critical for the doves, too thick and the doves will not cut out cleanly, too thin and the embossed detail will not be as prominent.

2 Take the dove cutter and repeatedly press it firmly into the rolled out paste as shown **(F)**. You will need approximately six per cake, depending on how you wish to arrange them.

Tip
If you are struggling to get a clean cut around the edges of the doves use a craft knife and carefully neaten them.

3 Liberally dust over each dove with the edible snowflake lustre dust to add shine and sparkle **(G)**.

The flowers and snowflakes

1 For the flowers, separately roll out the aqua, white and pale mid-green modelling paste between 1mm (1/32in) spacers and place under a stay fresh mat to prevent your rolled out paste from drying out.

2 Cut snowflakes from the white modelling paste, eight-petal flowers from the aqua paste and pale mid-green circles from the no.18 piping tube. You will need approximately six of each shape per cake. When using the flower cutter I often find it is easier to place the paste over the cutter as shown **(H)**, and roll over it with a rolling pin before turning the cutter over and releasing the paste flower with a paintbrush. Stack the shapes as shown, using a little sugar glue to secure **(I)**. Leave one snowflake for the top of the cake.

3 Using the photograph of my completed cake as a reference, attach the stacked flowers and doves to one of your covered tree cakes. Position the decorations so they disguise and soften the horizontal line of the base of the tree and leave parts of the tree undecorated to allow room for the scrolls. Add the prepared snowflake to the top of the tree.

DESIGNER

Tip
If you wish you can add movement to the doves by encouraging their wings or tail feathers to come away from the cake.

Adding the scrolls

1 Soften some of the dark blue-green modelling paste so it is really quite soft. Do this by first kneading in some white vegetable fat and then dunking the paste into cooled boiled water and re-kneading. Repeat until it feels soft and stretchy. Place the paste, together with the small round disc, into the sugar shaper.

2 Take a fine paintbrush and some sugar glue and paint freehand scrolls between the decorations on the cake **(J)**, referring to the pictures for guidance.

3 Squeeze out a length of paste from the sugar shaper (if the paste doesn't come out easily the paste isn't soft enough) and place it over a section of the painted glue pattern, using your fingers to aid placement **(K)**. Cut to size on the cake using a palette or craft knife. Review the shape and adjust as necessary, using a dry paintbrush to give the shape smooth curves. Repeat as required.

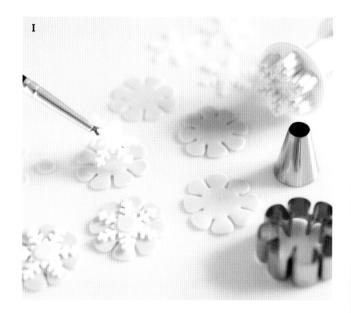

Adding the piped dots

1 Prepare your royal icing, adjusting the consistency so that you can easily pipe small dots not pointed cones. You want a freshly paddled smooth icing.

Tip

If you are making simple royal icing you may want to whiten it with some super-white dusting powder.

2 Place the no.1.5 piping tube into a small piping bag and half fill with royal icing. Supporting your hand, hold the tip fractionally above the surface of the cake. Squeeze the bag until you have a small dot, release the pressure and only then remove the tip, this helps avoid any unwanted peaks. Pipe groups of three dots in the spaces between the decoration **(L)**.

Decorating the white tree

The white tree is decorated in a very similar way but I have used different bird and flower cutters and have replaced the scrolls with piped lines of dots to represent tinsel.

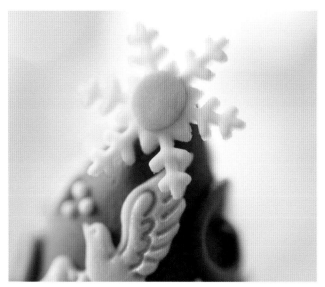

DESIGNER

Cosy Christmas

For a more jazzy Christmas, I have changed the colours of the trees to deep rich reds and oranges to give a sense of warmth and sumptuousness. I have also changed the decoration on one tree to give you more inspiration and ideas.

You will need

* **cake:** two 5cm (2in) round mini cakes for each tree
* **sugarpaste (rolled fondant):** red and orange
* **modelling paste:** red, pink, light orange and dark orange
* **cake board:** round hardboard, same size as your cakes, one per tree
* 2cm (¾in) wide wooden dowelling or similar for the trunk
* **cutters:** Lindy used 2.5cm (1in) Snowflake plunger cutter (PME), Lindy's eight-petal flat-ended petal flower from Flat Floral Collection set one (LC), Lindy's eight-petal pointed petal flower from Flat Floral Collection set one (LC), 2cm (¾in) and 1.3cm (⅝in) daisy Marguerite plunger cutters (PME), circle cutter – no.18 piping tube (PME), Lindy's small Chinese scroll cutter (LC), and Lindy's small stylized flower cutter (LC)
* lace motif embossing sticks – set 19 (HP)
* Daisy Mould Set – FL288 (FI)

> " Everything has beauty, but not everyone sees it. "
>
> Confucius

1 Carve and cover the cakes, as for the main cake, but this time using the red and orange sugarpaste. Make trunks and attach to the trees as before.

2 Create layered flowers as for the main cake and its variation. Then using the daisy mould and small balls of dark orange paste, make a selection of small orange daisies.

3 Thinly roll out the red modelling paste and emboss with a lace embosser. Then, using the smallest cutter from the stylized flower set, cut out embossed shapes. Pinch the base of each shape together and roll so the shape looks more like a four-fingered maple leaf. Next, thinly roll out the light orange modelling paste, emboss with a different lace embosser, then cut out shapes using the smallest cutter from the Chinese scroll set.

4 Attach all the above five elements to your trees. I have gone for a crowded busy look this time, making use of every available space, filling any gaps with the small daisies.

123

Equipment

You will find the following lists of equipment useful when baking and decorating your mini cakes. Specialist sugarcraft equipment, such as embossers, cutters and moulds, can be see in the step photography throughout the book.

Bowls in various sizes, for mixing (**1**)
Mini cake boards (**2**)
Baking parchment to line tins (**3**)
Wire rack for cooling (**4**)
Carving knives – sharp, long bladed pastry knives, for levelling cakes and carving shapes (**5**)
Cocktail sticks (toothpicks) used as a marker and to transfer small amounts of paste colour (**6**)
Measuring spoons for accurate measurement of ingredients (**7**)
Paintbrushes – in a range of sizes, useful for stippling, painting and dusting (**8**)
Piping tubes (tips) for piping, using in a sugar shaper and to cut small circles (**9**)
Rolling pins for rolling out the different types of paste (**10**)
Scissors for cutting templates and trimming paste to shape (**11**)
Set square for accurate alignment (**12**)
Spacers – 5mm and 1mm for rolling out paste (**13**)

Stay fresh mat for preventing rolled-out paste from drying out (**14**)
Multi-mini tins (pans) for baking mini cakes (**15**)
Multi-sized tin (pan) for baking squares for carved cakes (**16**)
Tools:
- Ball tool (FMM) to soften the edges of petals (**17**)

- Craft knife, for intricate cutting tasks **18**)

- Cutting wheel (PME) use instead of a knife to avoid dragging the paste (**19**)

- Dresden tool, to create markings on paste (**20**)

- Palette knife used for cutting and spreading (**21**)

> It's best to have your tools with you. If you don't you're apt to find something you didn't expect and get discouraged.
>
> Steven King

- Scriber (PME) for scribing around template, popping air bubbles in paste and removing small small sections of paste (**22**)

- Smoother helps create a smooth and even finish to sugarpaste (**23**)

- Sugar shaper and discs to create pieces of uniformly shaped modelling paste (**24**)

Work board – large and small, non-stick used for rolling out pastes (**25**)
Wooden spoon to help mix buttercream, ganache etc (**26**)
Pastry brush for spreading tasks, such as covering a fruit cake with apricot jam (**27**)

Measurements the world over

For readers who prefer to use US cup measurements, please use the following conversions (note: 1tbsp = 15ml but 1 Australian tbsp = 20ml):

Butter 115g (4oz) = 1 stick/½ cup, 225g (8oz) = 2 sticks/1cup, 25g (1oz) = 2 tbsp, 15g (½oz) = 1tbsp

Caster (superfine) sugar 200g (7oz) = 1 cup, 25g (1oz) = 2 tbsp

Plain (all-purpose flour)/self-raising (-rising) flour 125g (4½oz) = 1 cup

Icing (confectioners') sugar 115g (4oz) = 1 cup

Liquid 250ml (9fl oz) = 1 cup, 125ml (4fl oz) = ½ cup

Soft brown sugar 210g (7½oz) = 1 cup

Piping tubes

The following piping tubes (tips) have been used in the book. As the tube numbers may vary with different suppliers, always check the tube diameter:

Tube no. (PME)	Diameter
0	0.5mm (0.020in)
1	1mm (⅓₂in)
1.5	1.2mm (⅓₂in)
3	2mm (³⁄₃₂in)
16	5mm (³⁄₁₆in)
18	7mm (⁵⁄₃₂in)

Baking Mini Cakes

Mini cakes are great fun to bake and are ideal to give as presents. You can cut your mini cakes individually from larger cakes or use bakeware, such as a multi-mini cake tin (pan), that allows you to bake a number of small cakes at once. Alternatively, you can take the DIY approach and use food cans, oven proof dishes and even terracotta pots.

Lining tins

There are cake release sprays on the market which you can use, but I still prefer the traditional method of lining tins with baking paper (parchment), especially when using multi-mini tins. Neatly lined tins will prevent the cake mixture from sticking and help ensure a good shape. When using multi-mini tins lining each ring also means the cake batter can rise above the top edge allowing your mini cake height to be the same as its diameter. When lining tins, use a good quality paper that is designed for the purpose. The paper should always sit right up against the sides of the tin with no large air pockets. Watch the uppermost side edge of the lining paper, you do not want this going into the cake itself so secure with a little fat or a small fold in the paper.

Multi-mini tins

Line the base of the pan with an appropriately sized square of baking parchment, then cut strips of paper, slightly longer than the circumference of each mini cake mould and slightly higher. Place one paper strip inside each mould, so the sides of the strip overlap a little.

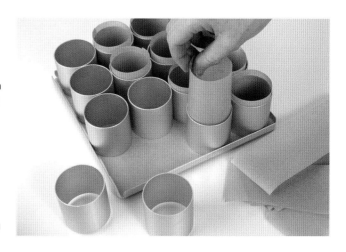

Square and rectangular

Measure the circumference of your tin and cut a strip of baking parchment slightly longer than this measurement to allow for an overlap. Make the strip 5cm (2in) deeper than the height of the tin. Fold up 2.5cm (1in) along the bottom of the strip. Crease the strip at intervals equal to the length of each of the inside edges of the tin, and then cut the folded section where it is creased into mitres. Grease the tin and place the strip around the sides with the cut edge on the base. Cut a piece of baking parchment to fit the base.

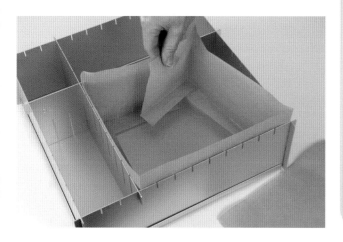

Baking tips

Use only the finest and freshest ingredients.

Use unsalted butter. Try not to use substitute fats, spreadable butters and low calorie spreads as these can often ruin a recipe as they have added air and water in them and so change the consistency of the mixture.

Make sure you measure your ingredients properly.

Mix the dry ingredients thoroughly before mixing in the liquids.

Always preheat your oven.

Ovens vary hugely so the amount of time a recipe takes to bake will depend on your oven. The secret is to get to know your oven and its settings, and perhaps buy yourself an oven thermometer so you can see the actual temperature at which you are baking.

Cake Recipes

The cake under the icing is vitally important – it needs to be moist, able to support the added weight of the icing and above all taste fantastic. Here is a collection of my tried and tested recipes for you to experiment with – enjoy!

Madeira cake

A firm, moist cake that can be flavoured to suit (see below). It is ideal for both carving and covering with sugarpaste, and will keep for up to two weeks.

Multi-mini round cake tins	16 x 5cm (2in) multi-mini round cakes	16 x 6.5cm (2½in) multi-mini round cakes	16 x 7.5cm (3in) multi-mini round cakes
Other tin shapes	18cm (7in) round or 15cm (6in) square 7.5cm (3in) deep cake	23cm (9in) round or 20cm (8in) square 7.5cm (3in) deep cake	28cm (11in) round or 25.5cm (10in) square 7.5cm (3in) deep cake
Unsalted butter	225g (8oz)	450g (1lb)	730g (1lb 9¾oz)
Caster (superfine) sugar	225g (8oz)	450g (1lb)	730g (1lb 9¾oz)
Self-raising flour	225g (8oz)	450g (1lb)	730g (1lb 9¾oz)
Plain (all-purpose) flour	125g (4½oz)	225g (8oz)	365g (12oz)
Large eggs	4	8	13
Baking times for mini cakes	40 minutes	50 minutes	1 hour

1 Preheat the oven to 160°C/140°C fan/325°F/Gas Mark 3. Grease and line the cake tins (pans) with baking paper (parchment).

2 Cream the butter and sugar in a large mixing bowl until light, fluffy and very pale, I find this takes about five minutes in a mixer. Sift the flours together in a separate bowl.

3 Beat the eggs, they should be at room temperature, into the creamed mixture, one at a time, following each with a spoonful of flour, to prevent the mixture curdling.

4 Sift the remaining flour into the creamed mixture and fold in carefully with a large metal spoon. Then add your choice of flavourings, if using.

5 Spoon or pipe the batter into your tins and bake until well risen, firm to the touch and a skewer inserted into the centre comes out clean. Adjust baking times according to your oven.

6 Leave the cakes to cool in the tins. Then, leaving the lining paper on, wrap the cake in foil or place in an airtight container for at least 12 hours before levelling, to allow the cake to settle.

Tip
Adjust times according to your particular oven.

Tip
Carefully break each egg into a cup to prevent small pieces of eggshell falling into the cake batter.

Flavourings

Traditionally, Madeira cake was flavoured with lemon, but it can be flavoured in many ways, here are a few for you to try. The amounts are given for a four-egg quantity Madeira cake; increase or decrease the amounts for other quantities.

- Lemon: grated zest of 2 lemons
- Vanilla: 5ml (1 tsp) vanilla extract
- Cherry: 250g (9oz) glacé (candied) cherries, halved
- Fruit: 250g (9oz) sultanas (golden raisins), currants, raisins or dates
- Coconut: 75g (3oz) desiccated (dry unsweetened shredded) coconut
- Almond: 5ml (1 tsp) almond essence (extract) and 30ml (2 tbsp) ground almonds

Chocolate cake

This rich, moist yet firm, chocolate cake is ideal for both carving and covering with sugarpaste and will keep for up to two weeks. The secret with this recipe is to use good quality chocolate with a reasonably high cocoa solids content. Don't be tempted to use cheap chocolate with low cocoa solids, or even supermarket baking chocolate, you simply will not achieve the rich depth of flavour that this cake demands!

Tip

A good way of transferring the cake batter to the multi-mini cake pans is to pipe the mixture using a large piping bag.

Multi-mini round cake tins	16 x 5cm (2in) multi-mini round cakes	16 x 6.5cm (2½in) multi-mini round cakes	16 x 7.5cm (3in) multi-mini round cakes
Other tin shapes	18cm (7in) round or 15cm (6in) square 7.5cm (3in) deep cake	23cm (9in) round or 20cm (8in) square 7.5cm (3in) deep cake	28cm (11in) round or 25.5cm (10in) square 7.5cm (3in) deep cake
Plain (bittersweet) chocolate	225g (8oz)	425g (15oz)	550g (1lb 4oz)
Unsalted butter	175g (6oz)	275g (9¾oz)	450g (1lb)
Caster (superfine) sugar	115g (4oz)	175g (6oz)	275g (9¾oz)
Large eggs	6	10	16
Icing sugar	40g (1½oz)	70g (2½oz)	115g (4oz)
Self raising flour	175g (6oz)	275g (9¾oz)	450g (1lb)
Baking times for mini cakes	30 minutes	45 minutes	1 hour

1 Preheat the oven to 180°C/160°C fan/350°F/Gas Mark 4. Grease and line the cake tins (pans) with baking paper (parchment).
2 Melt the chocolate, either in a double boiler or in a microwave. Cream the butter and sugar in a large mixing bowl until light, fluffy and pale.
3 Separate the eggs. Gradually add the egg yolks, then the melted chocolate. In a separate bowl, whisk the egg whites to soft peaks. Gradually whisk the icing sugar into the egg whites.
4 Sift the flour into another bowl and, using a large metal spoon, fold the flour alternately with the egg whites into the chocolate mixture.

5 Spoon or pipe the mixture into your lined bakeware, and bake. Baking times will depend on your oven, the cake tins used and the depth of the cake. When the cakes are baked they will be well risen, firm to the touch and a skewer inserted into the centre will come out clean. Adjust baking times according to your oven.
6 Allow the cakes to cool slightly then remove the baking rings and allow to cool completely. Once cool, wrap the cakes in foil or place in an airtight container for at least 12 hours before levelling, to allow the cake to settle.

Fruit cake

Rich fruit cake is a wonderful traditional cake packed full of candied and dried fruit, usually soaked in spirits and including nuts and spices. The quality of the fruit you use will make a huge difference to the flavour of your cake, so shop around to source the best you can find – candied peel you have to chop yourself is always much tastier. Fruit cake should be aged ideally for a least one month to allow the flavours to mature. If you prefer not to use spirits in your cake, try substituting apple or orange juice, or try grape or pomegranate. Note that without the alcohol preservative the cake won't last as long.

Multi-mini round cake tins	16 x 5cm (2in) multi-mini round cakes	16 x 6.5cm (2½in) multi-mini round cakes	16 x 7.5cm (3in) multi-mini round cakes
Other tin shapes	18cm (7in) round or 15cm (6in) square 7.5cm (3in) deep cake	23cm (9in) round or 20cm (8in) square 7.5cm (3in) deep cake	28cm (11in) round or 25.5cm (10in) square 7.5cm (3in) deep cake
Sultanas (golden raisins)	175g (6oz)	275g (10oz)	550g (1¼lb)
Currants	175g (6oz)	275g (10oz)	550g (1¼lb)
Raisins	175g (6oz)	275g (10oz)	550g (1¼lb)
Candied peel	75g (3oz)	150g (5oz)	275g (10oz)
Brandy	25ml (1½ tbsp)	37.5ml (2½ tbsp)	75ml (5 tbsp)
Plain (all-purpose) Flour	175g (6oz)	275g (10oz)	550g (1¼lb)
Ground almonds	40g (1½oz)	70g (2½oz)	150g (5oz)
Mixed (apple pie) spice	3.5ml (¾ tsp)	6.5ml (1¼ tsp)	12.5ml (2½ tsp)
Unsalted butter	175g (6oz)	275g (10oz)	550g (1¼lb)
Soft brown sugar	175g (6oz)	275g (10oz)	550g (1¼lb)
Eggs	3	5	10
Black treacle (blackstrap molasses)	15ml (1 tbsp)	20ml (4 tsp)	37.5ml (2½ tbsp)
Vanilla essence	2.5ml (½ tsp)	3.5ml (¾ tsp)	6.5ml (1¼ tsp)
Glacé (candied) cherries	75g (3oz)	150g (5oz)	275g (10oz)
Chopped almonds	40g (1½oz)	70g (2½oz)	150g (5oz)
Lemon rind and juice	¾	1¼	2½
Baking times for mini cakes (approx.)			
at 150°C	30 mins	1 hour	1 hour 15 minutes
at 120°C	30 mins	1 hour	1 hour 30 minutes

1 Soak the sultanas, currants, raisins and candied peel in brandy overnight.

2 Preheat the oven to 150°C/130°C fan/300°F/Gas Mark 2. Sieve the flour, spice and ground almonds into a bowl. In another bowl cream the butter and sugar until it is light, fluffy and pale, but do not over beat it.

3 Lightly mix together the eggs, treacle and vanilla, beat into the creamed mixture a little at a time, adding a spoonful of flour after each addition.

4 Rinse the cherries and chop, add to the fruit with the lemon rind and juice, chopped almonds and a small amount of flour. Fold the remaining flour into the creamed mixture, followed by the dried fruit. Add extra brandy or milk if necessary.

5 Carefully transfer your mixture into your lined bakeware and bake at 150°C/130°C fan/300°F/Gas Mark 2 for the stated cooking time and then reduce the temperature to 120°C/100°C fan/250°F/Gas Mark ½ and bake further for the time suggested. When the mini cakes are baked they will be firm to the touch and a skewer inserted into the centre will come out clean. Adjust baking times according to your oven. Allow the cakes to cool in the tin. You can add extra brandy to the cake while it is still cooling if you like. Prick the surface all over with a skewer and spoon some brandy over.

6 Leaving the lining paper on, wrap the cakes in baking parchment and then foil. Never store your cake in foil only, as the acid in the fruit will attack the foil. Store the cake in a cool, dry place. Fruit cake should be aged for at least one month to allow the flavour to mature.

Sticky toffee cakes

Moist and dense, rich and sweet with a beautiful flavour this recipe makes gorgeous mini cakes. These cakes are best eaten within five days.

Tip
Baked mini cakes can dry out quickly, so try not to leave them uncovered for any length of time.

Multi-mini round cake tins	16 x 5cm (2in) multi-mini round cakes	16 x 6.5cm (2½in) multi-mini round cakes	16 x 7.5cm (3in) multi-mini round cakes
Other tin shapes	18cm (7in) round or 15cm (6in) square 7.5cm (3in) deep cake	23cm (9in) round or 20cm (8in) square 7.5cm (3in) deep cake	28cm (11in) round or 25.5cm (10in) square 7.5cm (3in) deep cake
Butter	175g (6oz)	350g (12oz)	580g (1lb 5oz)
Dark brown soft sugar/muscovado	125g (4½oz)	250g (9oz)	415g (14¼oz)
Golden syrup	150g (5½oz)	300g (10½oz)	500g (1lb 2oz)
Black treacle (blackstrap molasses)	75g (2¾oz)	150g (5½oz)	250g (9oz)
Vanilla essence	1 tsp	2 tsp	3 tsp
Large eggs	3	6	10
Double (heavy) cream or creme fraiche	2 tbsp	4 tbsp	7 tbsp
Chopped dates	75g (2¾oz)	150g (5½oz)	250g (9oz)
Self-raising flour	200g (7oz)	400g (14oz)	670g (1lb 8oz)
Baking time for mini cakes	35 minutes	50 minutes	1 hour 10 minutes

1 Preheat oven to 180°C/ 160°C fan/ 350°F/ Gas 4. Line the cake tins (pans) with baking (parchment) paper.
2 Soften the butter so it is quite soft but not runny, I use a microwave to do this.
3 Place all the ingredients except the dates into a large mixing bowl and mix well. I use my electric mixer but a hand held whisk is fine.

4 Finally, stir in the chopped dates then place the batter into the mini cake tins, they should be about two thirds full and the dates evenly distributed.
5 Bake until risen and just set in middle or until a fine skewer inserted into the middle of a cake comes out clean. Leave to cool completely in the tin.

Orange and poppy seed cupcakes

I fell in love with this delicious cake on a teaching trip to Australia a few years ago. The tangy flavour and interesting texture of the poppy seeds and orange peel have me hooked! These cakes are best eaten within two weeks.

Tip

Home-made candied peel is always delicious and is not difficult to make. So why not have a go, then use it when baking these cakes - divine!

Multi-mini round cake tins	16 x 5cm (2in) multi-mini round cakes	16 x 6.5cm (2½in) multi-mini round cakes	16 x 7.5cm (3in) multi-mini round cakes
Other tin shapes	18cm (7in) round or 15cm (6in) square 7.5cm (3in) deep cake	23cm (9in) round or 20cm (8in) square 7.5cm (3in) deep cake	28cm (11in) round or 25.5cm (10in) square 7.5cm (3in) deep cake
Unsalted butter	185g (6¼oz)	370g (13oz)	620g (2lb ¼oz)
Caster (superfine) sugar	160g (5¾oz)	320g (11½oz)	530g (1lb 3oz)
Marmalade	100g (3½oz)	200g (7oz)	330g (11⅝oz)
Almond extract	¼ tsp	½ tsp	1 tsp
Orange zest from:	2 oranges	4 oranges	7 oranges
Orange juice	80ml (2¾fl oz)	160ml (5½fl oz)	270ml (9½fl oz)
Self-raising flour	185g (6¼oz)	370g (13lb)	620g (1lb 5¾oz)
Ground almonds	60g (3½oz)	120g (4⅛oz)	200g (7oz)
Poppy seeds	40g (1½oz)	80g (2⅞oz)	135g (4¾oz)
Candied peel	50g (1¾oz)	100g (3½oz)	170g (5⅞oz)
Large eggs	3	6	10
Baking time for mini cakes	30 minutes	45 minutes	1 hour

1 Preheat oven to 160°C/140°C fan/325°F/Gas Mark 3. Grease and line the cake tins (pans) with baking paper (parchment).
2 Place the butter, sugar, marmalade, almond essence, orange zest and juice in a pan and stir over low heat until the mixture is melted. Allow the mixture to cool.
3 Sift the flour, almonds and poppy seeds into a bowl, add the candied peel then make a well in the centre. Gradually pour the cooled liquid into the well and mix until smooth.

4 Add the lightly beaten eggs and mix until combined.
5 Pour the mixture into the lined tins. Bake until risen and just set in the middle or until a fine skewer inserted into the middle of the cake comes out clean. Adjust baking times according to your oven. Leave to cool completely in the tin.
6 Brush with an orange liquor, such as Cointreau, before icing.

Vegan chocolate cake

A perfect cake when you want to surprise someone who can't eat eggs or dairy. This cake has been a big hit with my blog readers and was developed with my son's egg allergic friend in mind – I always felt so mean not being able to offer him cake! The recipe makes quite a light cake but it is still strong enough to support sugarpaste. I like it covered in chocolate ganache, but remember this may need to be vegan.

Tip
To make a vegan ganache, substitute the cream with thick coconut milk.

	16 x 5cm (2in) multi-mini round cakes	16 x 6.5cm (2½in) multi-mini round cakes	16 x 7.5cm (3in) multi-mini round cakes
Multi-mini round cake tins			
Other tin shapes	18cm (7in) round or 15cm (6in) square 7.5cm (3in) deep cake	23cm (9in) round or 20cm (8in) square 7.5cm (3in) deep cake	28cm (11in) round or 25.5cm (10in) square 7.5cm (3in) deep cake
Plain (all purpose) flour	260g (9¼oz)	520g (1lb 2¾oz)	870g (2lb)
Muscovado/dark brown sugar	250g (9oz)	500g (1lb 2oz)	840g (1lb 14oz)
Cocoa powder (unsweetened cocoa)	4 tbsp	8 tbsp	13½ tbsp
Bicarbonate of soda (baking soda)	1¼ tsp	2½ tsp	3¾ tsp
Water	300ml (10fl oz)	615ml (1 pint)	1 litre (1¾ pints)
Sunflower oil	120ml (4⅜fl oz)	250ml (9fl oz)	400ml (14fl oz)
Balsamic vinegar	1tbsp	2.5tbsp	4tbsp
Vanilla essence	1tsp	1½tsp	4tsp
Baking time for mini cakes	30 minutes	40 minutes	50 minutes

1 Preheat oven to 180°C/160°C fan/350°F/Gas Mark 4. Grease and carefully line the cake tins (pans) with baking paper (parchment). Note: the batter is quite runny so make sure the lining paper is a good fit.
2 Sift the flour, sugar, cocoa powder and bicarbonate of soda into a bowl and mix together
3 Make a well in the centre and add the remaining liquid ingredients and stir until just combined.

4 Carefully pour the batter into the lined tins. Each tin should be about two thirds full.
5 Bake in the pre-heated oven until a fine skewer inserted one of the central cakes comes out clean. Adjust the baking times according to your oven. Cool the for five minutes before removing them to a wire rack to cool completely.

Sugar Recipes

Most of the sugar recipes used in the book for covering, modelling and decoration can easily be made at home.

Sugarpaste

Used to cover cakes ready-made sugarpaste (rolled fondant) can be obtained from supermarkets and cake-decorating suppliers, and is available in white and the whole colour spectrum. It is also easy and inexpensive to make your own.

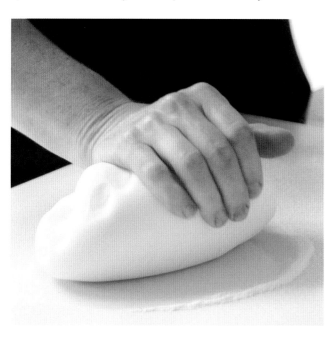

Makes 1kg (2¼lb)

* ✳ 60ml (4tbsp) cold water
* ✳ 20ml (4tsp or 1 sachet) powdered gelatine
* ✳ 125ml (4fl oz) liquid glucose
* ✳ 15ml (1tbsp) glycerine
* ✳ 1kg (2¼lb) icing (confectioners') sugar (sieved) plus extra for dusting

1 Place the water in a small bowl, sprinkle over the gelatine and soak until spongy. Stand the bowl over a pan of hot but not boiling water and stir until the gelatine is dissolved. Add the glucose and glycerine, stirring until well blended and runny.
2 Put the icing sugar in a large bowl. Make a well in the centre and slowly pour in the liquid ingredients, stirring constantly. Mix well. Turn out on to a surface dusted with icing sugar and knead until smooth, sprinkling with extra icing sugar if the paste becomes too sticky. The paste can be used immediately or tightly wrapped and stored in a plastic bag until required.

Modelling paste

Used to add decoration to cakes, this versatile paste keeps its shape well, dries harder than sugarpaste. Although there are commercial pastes available, it is easy and a lot cheaper to make your own.

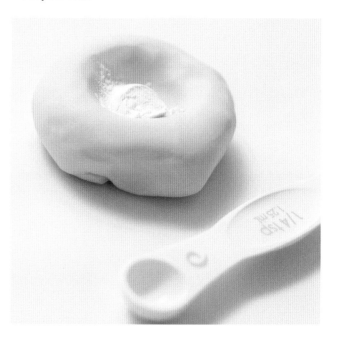

Makes 225g (8oz)

* ✳ 225g (8oz) sugarpaste (rolled fondant)
* ✳ 5ml (1tsp) gum tragacanth

1 Make a well in the sugarpaste and add the gum tragacanth, then knead in.
2 Wrap in a plastic bag and allow the gum to work before use. You will begin to feel a difference in the paste after an hour or so, but it is best left overnight. The modelling paste should be firm but pliable with a slight elastic texture. Kneading the modelling paste makes it warm and easy to work with.

Tips

If your paste is crumbly or too hard to work, add a touch of white vegetable fat (shortening) and a little boiled water, and knead until softened.

If time is short use CMC instead of gum traganth; this is a synthetic product but it works almost straight away.

Placing your modelling paste in a microwave for a few seconds is an excellent way of warming it for use.

Pastillage

Used to make sugar pieces that extend above or to the side of a cake. This is an extremely useful paste because, unlike modelling paste, it sets extremely hard and is not affected by moisture the way other pastes are. However, the paste crusts quickly and is brittle once dry. You can buy it in a powdered form, to which you add water, but it is easy to make yourself.

Makes 350g (12oz)

* 1 egg white
* 300g (11oz) icing (confectioners') sugar (sifted)
* 10ml (2tsp) gum tragacanth

1 Put the egg white into a large mixing bowl. Gradually add enough icing sugar until the mixture combines together into a ball. Mix in the gum tragacanth, and then turn the paste out on to a work board or work surface and knead the pastillage well.
2 Incorporate the remaining icing sugar into the remainder of pastillage to give a stiff paste. Store pastillage in a polythene bag placed in an airtight container in a refrigerator for up to one month.

Flower paste (petal/gum paste)

Used to make delicate sugar flowers, flower paste is available commercially from sugarcraft suppliers and can be bought in white and a variety of colours. There are many varieties available so try a few to see which you prefer. Alternatively, it is possible to make your own but it is a time-consuming process and you will need a heavy-duty mixer.

Makes 500g (1lb 2oz)

* 500g (1lb 2oz) icing (confectioners') sugar
* 15ml (1tbsp) gum tragacanth
* 25ml (1½tbsp) cold water
* 10ml (2tsp) powered gelatine
* 10ml (2tsp) liquid glucose
* 15ml (1tbsp) white vegetable fat (shortening)
* 1 medium egg white

1 Sieve the icing sugar and gum tragacanth into the greased mixing bowl of a heavy-duty mixer (the grease eases the strain on the machine).
2 Place the water in a small bowl, sprinkle over the gelatine and soak until spongy. Stand the bowl over a pan of hot but not boiling water and stir until the gelatine is dissolved. Add the glucose and white vegetable fat to the gelatine and continue heating until all the ingredients are melted and mixed.

3 Add the glucose mixture and egg white to the icing sugar. Beat the mixture very slowly until mixed – at this stage it will be a beige colour – then increase the speed to maximum until the paste becomes white and stringy.
4 Grease your hands and remove the paste from the bowl. Pull and stretch the paste several times, and then knead together. Place in a plastic bag and store in an airtight container. Leave the paste to mature for at least 12 hours.

Tips

Flower paste dries quickly, so when using only cut off only as much as you need and reseal the remainder.

Work it well with your fingers, it should 'click' between your fingers when it is ready to use.

If it is too hard and crumbly, add a little egg white and white vegetable fat (shortening) – the fat slows down the drying process and the egg white makes it more pliable.

Buttercream

Buttercream has many uses, in this book I use it to fill between layers of cake and to crumb coat and act as a glue for sugarpaste. There are quite a few different recipes, but this standard recipe is very easy to make.

Makes 450g (1lb)

* 110g (3 ¾oz) unsalted butter
* 350g (12oz) icing (confectioners') sugar
* 15–30ml (1–2 tbsp) milk or water
* a few drops of vanilla extract or alternative flavouring

1 Place the butter in a bowl and beat until light and fluffy. Sift the icing sugar into the bowl and continue to beat until the mixture changes colour.
2 Add just enough milk or water to give a firm but spreadable consistency. Flavour by adding the vanilla or alternative flavouring, then store the buttercream in an airtight container until required.

Chocolate ganache

Used as a filling or coating, ganache is ideal for coating mini cakes as it sets firm and so makes covering mini cakes with sugarpaste easier. A must for all chocoholics – use the best chocolate you can source.

Dark chocolate ganache:

Makes 400g (14oz)

* 200g (7oz) good-quality dark (bittersweet) chocolate
* 200ml (7fl oz) cream

White chocolate ganache:

Makes 280g (9½oz)

* 200g (7oz) good-quality white chocolate
* 80ml (2½fl oz) cream

1 Melt the chocolate and cream together in a bowl over a saucepan of gently simmering water, stirring to combine. Alternatively use a microwave on low power, stirring thoroughly every 20 seconds or so.
2 Place in the fridge to cool so that it can be easily spread with a palette knife.

Quick royal icing

Use this recipe for quick and easy tasks when only a little royal icing is required or when you need a strong 'glue'.

* 1 large egg white
* 250g (9oz) icing (confectioners') sugar (sifted)

1 Put the egg white in a bowl, lightly beat to break it down then gradually beat in the icing sugar until the icing is glossy and forms soft peaks.
2 Store your royal icing in an airtight container, cover the top surface with plastic film and then a clean damp cloth to prevent the icing forming a crust, before adding the lid and placing in a refrigerator.
3 Before using bring to room temperature and paddle the icing on your work board with a palette knife to remove any trapped air bubbles.

Professional royal icing

For intricate piping details it's well worth going to the effort of making professional icing, even though you will need to prepare the egg whites the day before. Use this recipe for the 'Fair Isle and Beyond' cakes.

* 90g (3oz) free range egg white (approx 3 eggs)
* 455g (1lb) icing (confectioners') sugar (sifted)
* 5–7 drops of lemon juice, if using fresh eggs

1 Separate the egg whites the day before needed, sieve through a fine sieve or tea strainer, cover and then place in a refrigerator to allow the egg white to strengthen.
2 Make sure all your equipment is spotless, even small residues of grease will affect your icing.
3 Place the egg whites into the bowl of a mixer, stir in the icing sugar and add the lemon juice.
4 Using the whisk attachment, turn the machine on and beat as slowly as possible for between 10 and 20 minutes, until the icing makes soft peaks. How long this takes will depend on your mixer. Take care not to over mix but test by lifting a little icing out of the bowl, if the icing forms a peak that bends over slightly it is the correct consistency.

Tip
You can substitute dried albumen for fresh egg whites if you prefer.

5 Store your royal icing in an airtight container, cover the top surface with plastic film and then a clean damp cloth to prevent the icing from forming a crust, before adding the lid and placing it in a refrigerator. Bring to room temperature before using again.

Glues

You can often just use water to stick your sugar decorations to your cakes. However, if you find you need something a little stronger here are two options.

Sugar glue

This is a quick, easy, instant 'glue' to make and is my preferred choice. Break up pieces of white modelling paste into a small container and cover with boiling water. Stir until dissolved. This produces a thick, strong glue, which can be easily thinned by adding some more cooled boiled water.

If a stronger glue is required, use pastillage rather than modelling paste as the base. This is particularly useful for delicate work.

White vegetable fat

This is a solid white vegetable fat (shortening) that is often known by a brand name: in the UK, Trex; in South Africa, Holsum; in Australia, Copha; and in America, Crisco. These products are more or less interchangeable in cake making.

Apricot glaze

This glaze is traditionally used to stick marzipan to fruit cakes. You can also use other jams or jellies, such as apple jelly. Redcurrant jelly is delicious on chocolate cakes when a marzipan covering is used. Place 115g (4oz) apricot jam and 30ml (2tbsp) of water into a pan. Heat gently until the jam has melted, and then boil rapidly for 30 seconds. Strain through a sieve if pieces of fruit are present. Use warm.

Covering Mini Cakes

Follow these basic techniques to achieve a neat and professional appearance to the initial cake coverings. With care and practise you will soon find that you have a perfectly smooth finish.

BASICS

Levelling the cakes

Making an accurate cake base is an important part of creating your sweet mini treat. For cakes baked in multi-mini cake tins (pans) simply place the cakes back into the baking rings and, with a sharp knife, cut the tops of the cakes level, using the top of the tin as a guide **(A)**. This will ensure the cake is completely level.

Filling cakes

It is not necessary to add fillings to the cake recipes used in this book. However, many people like to add complementary flavours and fill their cakes with say, chocolate and orange ganache, praline buttercream or delicious home-made lemon curd. To add a filling, split the cake into a number of horizontal layers and add the filling. Set in a fridge if appropriate. When choosing fillings, bear in mind that your little cakes have to support the weight of the sugarpaste and the decoration, so thin layers or layers that set firm are preferable **(B)**.

Freezing cakes

This allows you not only to bake your cakes in advance but also to fill and carve the cakes more easily without the cake crumbling and falling apart. Freezing cake is also ideal when you only require one or two mini cakes at a time.

Covering a cake with buttercream

A buttercream covering or crumb coat, is the traditional way to prepare a sponge cake that is to be covered with sugarpaste. The buttercream layer helps create an even surface and seals in the crumbs.

1 Attach a mini cake to a board, the same size as the cake, using a little buttercream.
2 Beat your buttercream until it is of a soft and spreadable consistency.
3 Using a palette knife cover the cake with a thin layer of buttercream, filling in any holes to create a smooth surface on which to place the sugarpaste layer.

Tip
Apply just before covering a cake with sugarpaste so the buttercream acts as a glue.

Covering a cake with chocolate ganache

This is a delicious alternative to buttercream, especially when using a chocolate cake. The great advantage of using ganache on mini sponge cakes is that it sets firmly and so adds stability to the cakes, making them easier to cover in sugarpaste. The disadvantage is that it takes a little longer to apply as the two layers of ganache have to set.

1 Make your ganache and allow it to set.
2 Mix and soften the ganache until it is smooth and easily spreads. If your ganache is too hard, place it in a microwave for a few seconds at a time to help soften it.
3 Attach a mini cake to a board, the same size as the cake, using a little ganache. Place in a freezer for a few minutes to set.
4 Using a palette knife, roughly cover the sides and top with a thick layer of ganache, making sure there are no air pockets **(A)**. Take off the excess with a side scraper or set square **(B)**, bringing in the excess ganache from the top edge onto the top of the cake. Place in a freezer for a few minutes to set.
5 Add a second layer, ensuring that the finish is perfectly smooth, the cake sides are vertical and the top is level **(C)**. Set in a freezer.
6 To attach sugarpaste to a ganached cake simply brush hot water, sugar syrup, which can be flavoured, or piping gel over the cake to act as glue.

A

B

Tip
Use a white chocolate ganache for cakes to be covered with a light-coloured sugarpaste.

C

Covering a cake with marzipan

Baked mini fruit cakes should be covered with marzipan before the sugarpaste covering is applied, to add flavour, to seal in the moisture and to prevent the fruit staining the sugarpaste.

1 Cover the top of a board the same size as your mini cake with a very thin layer of marzipan. Place your cake upside down on the covered board so that the flatter surface (the base), becomes the top **(A)**. This layer of marzipan prevents the fruit cake from sitting directly on the board, as the acid in the fruit will dissolve the silver covering.

2 Knead the marzipan so that it becomes supple; do not over-knead as this changes its consistency.

3 Brush the cake with warm apricot glaze and use small pieces of marzipan to fill any holes in the cake. Roll out the marzipan between some 5mm (¼in) spacers, using icing (confectioners') sugar or white vegetable fat (shortening) to stop it sticking to your work surface. Turn the marzipan around whilst rolling to maintain an appropriate shape, but do not turn it over.

4 Lift up the marzipan over a rolling pin and place over the mini cake **(B)**. Smooth the top of the cake with a smoother and then, using a cupped hand and an upward movement, encourage the marzipan on the sides of the cake to adjust to the shape of your cake **(C)**. Do not press down on any pleats in the paste, instead open them out and redistribute the paste.

5 Smooth the top curved edge with the palm of your hand and the sides with a smoother. Gradually press down with the smoother around the edge of the cake into the excess marzipan, and then trim this away to create a neat edge.

6 You may find that the marzipan is thicker at the bottom of the cake than the top, to help overcome this, rotate the cake between to two flat edged smoothers to redistribute the paste and ensure the sides of the cake are vertical.

7 You should allow the marzipan to harden in a warm, dry place for 24–48 hours before decorating the cake. Just before covering with sugarpaste, brush clear alcohol, for example gin or vodka, over the surface of the marzipan to act as a glue.

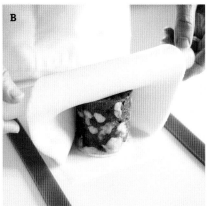
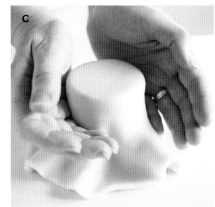

A B C

Mini cake size	Marzipan and sugarpaste quantities 5mm (¼in) thickness		
	One cake	Two cakes	For each additional cake
5cm (2in) round	90g (3¼oz)	150g (5½oz)	+ 60g (2¼oz)
6.5cm (2½in) round	175g (6oz)	275g (9¾oz)	+100g (3½oz)
7.5cm (3in) round	300g (10½oz)	450g (1lb)	+150g (5½oz)
Paisley	85g (3oz)	150g (5½oz)	+65g (2⅜oz)
Beach hut	330g (11½oz)	500g (1lb 2oz)	+170g (6oz)
Pocket watch	80g (2⅞oz)	125g (5oz)	+45g (1⅝oz)
6.5cm (2½in) cube Teddy surprise	350g (12oz)	590g (1lb 5oz)	+240g (9oz)
5cm (2in) cube	130g (5¼oz)	205g (7⅛oz)	+75g (2¾oz)
Baby bottle	220g (4⅜oz)	360g (12¼oz)	+140g (5oz)
Tree	220g (4⅜oz)	335g (11¾oz)	+115g (4oz)

Marzipan and sugarpaste quantities

Use this chart to help you estimate how much sugarpaste or marzipan you are going to need. The first mini cake always requires the most marzipan or sugarpaste as you will be able to re-use the trimmings when covering additional cakes. But watch out – if you find your trimmings are not re-usable you will need to allow more paste!

Covering a cake with sugarpaste

Once your cake is covered with buttercream, ganache or marzipan it is ready to be covered in sugarpaste.

1 Knead the sugarpaste until warm and pliable. Roll out on a surface lightly smeared with white vegetable fat (shortening), rather than icing (confectioners') sugar. White vegetable fat works well, and you don't have the problems of icing sugar drying out or marking the sugarpaste. Roll the paste to a depth of 5mm (¼in). It is a good idea to use spacers for this, as they ensure an even thickness.
2 Lift the paste carefully over the top of the cake, supporting it with a rolling pin, and position it so that it covers the cake. Smooth the top surface of the cake to remove any lumps and bumps using a smoother. Smooth the top edge using the palm of your hand.

Tip
Always make sure your hands are clean and dry with no traces of cake crumbs before smoothing sugarpaste.

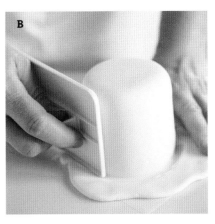

3 Using a cupped hand and an upward movement encourage the sugarpaste on the sides of the cake to adjust to the shape of your cake **(A)**. Do not press down on any pleats in the paste, instead open them out and redistribute the paste, until the cake is completely covered. Smooth the sides using a smoother.
4 Take the smoother and while pressing down, run the flat edge around the base of the cake to create a cutting line **(B)**. Trim away the excess paste with a palette knife to create a neat edge.
5 You may find that the sugarpaste is thicker at the bottom of the mini cake than the top. To help overcome this problem, rotate the mini cake between to two flat-edged smoothers to redistribute the paste and ensure the sides of the cake are vertical **(C)**.

Tip
If you find you have unwanted air bubbles under the icing, insert a scriber at an angle and press out the air.

Storage

Protect your decorated mini cakes by placing them on a cake board in a clean, covered cardboard cake box, and store somewhere cool and dry but never in a fridge. If the mini cakes are to be transported, place non-slip matting under the cakes to prevent them moving.

The following conditions will affect your decorated mini cakes:

- Sunlight will fade and alter the colours of icing, so always store in a dark place.
- Humidity can have a disastrous effect on modelling paste decorations, causing the icing to become soft and to droop if free standing. It can also causes dark colours to bleed into lighter colours.
- Heat can melt icing, especially buttercream, and prevent sugarpaste crusting over.

Giving and displaying mini cakes

These delightfully tiny treats make superb edible gifts. Simply place them in small transparent boxes tied up with bows or wrap in cellophane tied with suitable ribbons.

For birthdays or celebrations, present these pretty cakes individually on elegant vintage saucers or exquisite mini cake stands. For larger celebrations, group a collection of mini cakes onto delicate plates or perhaps sophisticated multi-tiered cake stands as a perfect alternative to a traditional wedding cake or as part of a dessert table.

About the author

Well known and highly respected in the sugarcraft industry, Lindy Smith has over 20 years' experience in sugarcrafting. Lindy is a designer who likes to share her love of sugarcraft and inspire fellow enthusiasts by writing books and teaching. Lindy is the author of 13 cake decorating titles for D&C the most recent including: *Creative Colour for Cake Decorating*, which won an International Gourmand Cookbook award for Best Pastry Sweet Book in the UK, 2014, Lindy's bestselling *The Contemporary Cake Decorating Bible*, *Bake Me I'm Yours....Cupcake Celebration*, *Bake Me I'm Yours Cookie*, *Cakes to Inspire and Desire* and *Party Animal Cakes*.

Lindy's teaching takes her all around the world, giving her the opportunity to educate and inspire, while also learning about local traditions and cake decorating issues. This knowledge is ultimately then fed back into her work. She has appeared on television many times and presented a sugarcraft series on Good Food Live. Lindy also heads Lindy's Cakes Ltd, a well-established business that runs her online shop, www.lindyscakes.co.uk, and her cake decorating workshops both in the UK and abroad. In 2012, Lindy won *Insight Magazine's* Business Woman of the Year. Katherine Benson, the magazine editor, said: "Lindy Smith is a remarkable woman. Not only does she boast high-level skills to create her own designs, but she thrives on helping others achieve their goals when it comes to making that cake not only taste good but look good too. Her range of knowledge is extensive and from her website to her books, cutters and stencils and classes, Lindy has shown that being business savvy isn't all about profiting yourself, but also about profiting others too".

To see what Lindy is currently doing, become a fan of Lindy's Cakes on Facebook or follow Lindy on Twitter. For baking advice and a wealth of information, visit her blog via the Lindy's Cakes website: www.lindyscakes.co.uk

Acknowledgments

Creating a book is never an easy task, it takes a lot of time and effort, and finding the time with this particular book has been a challenge. I am however thrilled with the outcome, I never imaged when I started that it would look quite so beautiful. This was meant to be a 'quick book' but once started I couldn't contain it, my imagination and creativity got the better of me!

I would therefore like to thank my wonderful husband, Graham for his support, especially as we moved our home 150 miles across the country whilst this book was being written. I would like to thank Jack Kirby from Bang Wallop for yet more stunning photos – it was a pleasure working with you Jack. To see more of Jack's wonderful shots, take a look at my award-winning *Creative Colour for Cake Decorating* book. A huge thank you goes to my daughter, Charlotte, who willingly gave up precious days of her Easter holidays to create many of the beautiful mood board backgrounds. Finally, I'd like to thank the team at my publishers for allowing me a huge amount of creative freedom, for letting me develop and implement my ideas to create this unique and magical book.

Suppliers

UK

Lindy's Cakes Ltd (LC)
Brandhill, Onibury, Craven Arms, Shropshire SY7 0PG
www.lindyscakes.co.uk
Manufacturer of cutters and
stencils plus online shop for
equipment used in this and
Lindy's other books.

Alan Silverwood Ltd
Ledsam House, Ledsam Street, Birmingham B16 8DN
Tel: +44(0)121 454 3571
www.alansilverwood.co.uk
Manufacturer of multi-sized cake pans, multi-mini cake pans
and spherical moulds/ball tins.

FMM Sugarcraft (FMM)
*Unit 7, Chancerygate Business Park, Whiteleaf Road, Hemel
Hempstead, Hertfordshire HP3 9HD*
Telephone: +44(0)1442 292970
www.fmmsugarcraft.com
Manufacturer of cutters.

Holly Products (HP)
*Primrose Cottage, Church Walk, Norton in Hales,
Shropshire TF9 4QX*
Tel / Fax +44(0)1630 655759
www.hollyproducts.co.uk
Manufacturer and supplier of embossing sticks and moulds.

Patchwork Cutter (PC)
*Unit 12, Arrowe Commercial Park, Arrowe Brook Road,
Upton, Wirral CH49 1AB*
Tel/Fax: +44(0)151 678 5053
www.patchworkcutters.co.uk
Manufacturers and supplier of cutters and embossers.

US

Global Sugar Art
1509 Military Turnpike, Plattsburgh, NY 12901
1-518-561-3039
1-800-420-6088
www.globalsugarart.com
Sugarcraft supplier that imports many UK products to the US.

Cake Craft Shoppe
3554 Highway 6, Sugar Land, Texas 77478
281-491-3920
www.cakecraftshoppe.com

First Impressions Molds (FI)
*300 Business Park Way, Suite A-200, Royal Palm Beach,
FL 33411*
561-784-7186
www.firstimpressionsmolds.com

Australia

Iced Affair
53 Church Street, Camperdown, NSW 2050
(02) 9519 3679
www.icedaffair.com.au

Abbreviations used in this book

DS – Designer Stencils
FI – First Impressions
FMM – FMM Sugarcraft
GI – Great Impressions
HP – Holly Products
JEM – JEM cutter cc
LC – Lindy's Cakes Ltd
PC – Patchwork cutters
PME – PME sugarcraft

SUPPLIERS

Index

A DAVID & CHARLES BOOK
© F&W Media International, Ltd 2014

David & Charles is an imprint of F&W Media International, Ltd
Brunel House, Forde Close, Newton Abbot, TQ12 4PU, UK

F&W Media International, Ltd is a subsidiary of F+W Media, Inc
10151 Carver Road, Suite #200, Blue Ash, OH 45242, USA

Text and Designs © Lindy Smith 2014
Layout and Photography © F&W Media International, Ltd 2014

First published in the UK and USA in 2014

A catalogue record for this book is available from the British Library.

ISBN-13: 978-1-4463-0407-5 hardback
ISBN-10: 1-4463-0407-8 hardback

ISBN-13: 978-1-4463-0408-2 paperback
ISBN-10: 1-4463-0408-6 paperback

Printed in China by RR Donnelley for:
F&W Media International, Ltd
Brunel House, Forde Close, Newton Abbot, TQ12 4PU, UK

10 9 8 7 6 5 4 3 2 1

Acquisitions Editor: Ame Verso
Editor: Emma Gardner
Project Editor: Jane Trollope
Art Editor: Charly Bailey
Photographer: Jack Kirby
Production Manager: Beverley Richardson

F+W Media publishes high quality books on a wide range of subjects.
For more great book ideas visit: www.stitchcraftcreate.co.uk